AF488312

We Need to Talk About Sin

"See to it, brothers and sisters, that none of you has a sinful, unbelieving heart that turns away from the living God. But encourage one another daily, as long as it is called 'Today,' so that none of you may be hardened by sin's deceitfulness"

Hebrews 3:12-13

Table of Contents

We Need to Talk About Sin

About Sin

Noah Shaw

Preface

At the time of writing this introduction, I am around a month away from graduating from college. I attend a Christian university. I am surrounded by Christians. I have classes with Christian professors. I attend Christian chapel services put on by the school. One may think that to be surrounded by faith on a daily basis would be empowering and uplifting to my spiritual life. In many ways it has been. I have also had my heart broken for the sake of my peers and campus multiple times. I have seen friends enter as freshmen with a strong and growing faith, only to have that faith in shambles four years later. I have heard more profanity in the past four years come from Christians than unbelievers. I have seen Christians consume sin-saturated media without a second thought. I have seen those who have never repented live under a false assurance of salvation. I have seen alcohol abuse and sexual sin run rampant in the lives of my peers, and those in spiritual leadership refuse to speak against it. I have seen the doctrines of sin and hell ignored and downplayed by those in spiritual authority. I have seen professors deny that Christ died for our sins. I have reason for my heart to break, and reason to cry. Both have happened on many occasions.

A big motivation for writing this book is that I do not believe my campus to be unique. I do not believe that it is only at my school where sin runs rampant, unbelievers are given false assurance of salvation, and important doctrines are abandoned. These things are happening in churches, Christian schools, and more, all across the country. It is heartbreaking that sin is destroying the lives of many Christians, that unbelievers are being comforted as they walk the path toward hell, and that many of those in spiritual leadership do not want to acknowledge these realities. It is tragic how many people are a heartbeat away from an eternity in hell with nobody to warn them. Yet, the indifference of Christians to this fact is even more heartbreaking. I am appalled by the indifference of Christian leaders. I am appalled by the indifference of many of my peers. I am appalled by the indifference that I find in my own life. I am heartbroken that I am not more heartbroken.

I wrote this book as a call. A call to Christians, pastors, and ministers, but most importantly a call to my own university. If I could summarize the biggest need my campus faces, it is the need to talk about sin, the sinfulness of mankind, and God's eternal punishment of sin. I believe that this is the biggest need in many other places as well. I publish this book heartbroken over what I have seen yet praying that God will raise up those who will call sinners to repentance and point them to forgiveness in Christ. I hope this book finds you well, and that you benefit from it.

Sincerely,

Noah Shaw

Introduction

Does This Even Matter?

Falling short. Rebellion against God. Transgression of God's law. Sin. I believe that in the Christian world, sin must be talked about. After all, that is the premise of this book, a premise that many will be quick to question. There is a genuine question many will have concerning to the topic of this book: Does it even matter? Does it matter if we talk about sin? Is it a big deal if we push this doctrine to the side and ignore it? Does it matter if we even believe in sin to begin with? My response to all these questions is an overwhelmingly emphatic yes. We need to talk about sin, and denial of that doctrine has large consequences. It is becoming increasingly unpopular to believe in things such as sin, a God who punishes sin, and the inherent sinfulness of man, yet these key doctrines are foundational to Christianity.

Those who read this book will likely come from different backgrounds, whether that be differing theological traditions or different religions altogether. I believe that all of us have a sinful nature. That nature leads us to sin, and because we have sinned, we face the judgment of God for our sins in a place called hell. There will be many self-professing Christians who disagree with that statement. If you are one of them, I hope to demonstrate how denying those things leads to the creation of a false Jesus, the deterioration of Christianity, and the destruction of any biblically based faith you may believe that you hold.

There will also be many Christians who agree with the statement but disagree with how it was phrased. It may scare some people off or stir up sorrow if we tell them that they are sinners. Instead of saying that "because of our sins we face hell, so repent and trust in Christ," we should replace that statement with "let Jesus restore your internal brokenness so that you may experience newness of life." If you are one of these people, I hope to demonstrate how euphemizing these key doctrines has terrible consequences, how watering down or hiding key doctrines behind flowery language is anything but a beneficial idea.

There will also be many who wonder what the big deal is. Does ignoring or denying the doctrines of sin, sinful man, and hell, have any real-world implications? For those people, as well as everyone else, I hope to demonstrate that it truly is important to talk about sin. As we will see, we need to talk about sin because sin is real, and conviction is important. There are real life consequences to the words we use, and we will be held responsible for those very words. Furthermore, the Christian faith crumbles without a just God who will punish sinful man in the next life. I hope you enjoy this book and learn a little bit about why *We Need to Talk About Sin*.

Chapter 1

Sin is Real

In Genesis 3, we encounter the reality of sin and witness it entering the world. When told to abstain from the Tree of the Knowledge of Good and Evil, Adam and Eve disobeyed God. They believed the lies of the serpent and ate from the tree. From that point on, the world was cursed with the existence of sin and all the consequences it brings along. One of those consequences is death. Sin brings death, and "just as sin entered the world through one man, and death through sin … in this way death came to all people, because all sinned" (Romans 5:12). Sin destroys. It brings pain and warps things that were previously good into that which is evil. It is not simply an abstract concept, but a present reality of the world we live in. Our society is rampant with sin, and many Christians have become immune and numb to that which is an offense and abomination to God. Because of that, it is proper to begin with an overview of sin, its presence in the world, and the destruction that it brings.

Sin is Expansive

The issue of sin reaches far wider than any of us can imagine. Sin reaches far deeper into our soul than we would like to admit and is found in many more of our actions than we would like to believe. James gives us one of the harshest yet most expansive definitions of sin when he writes that "if anyone, then, knows the good they ought to do and doesn't do it, it is sin for them" (James 4:17). Many people believe that sinning is simply breaking one of a few rules found in the Bible. James destroys the narrative that sin is relegated to a small list of actions, but instead shows us that sinning is not only doing the wrong thing, but failing to do the right thing as well. Because of this, sin is far more present in our lives than we could ever imagine. We sin when we intentionally do what is wrong. We sin when we fall into wrongdoing without knowing it. We sin when we know what is right and refuse to do it.

In Romans, Paul also tells us about those who "invent ways of doing evil" (Romans 1:30). Not only do we sin more than we like to believe, but some people actively find new ways to sin. While "inventing evil" may seem far-fetched, a look at modern culture shows that new forms of evil are invented every single day. Popular TV shows are filled with explicit sexual content and unnecessarily gory violence, with new episodes airing every week. Music artists become popular by singing about the various sexual acts they take part in. New types of illegal and dangerous drugs are regularly invented and flooded into our cities. If you want to find a new way to sin, a new way to disobey God, it would not be very hard. Sin is something that permeates every aspect of our culture and our own lives. God told Cain that "sin is crouching at your door; it desires to have you" (Genesis 4:7). The same is true of us. Sin is everywhere in the world, trying to draw us in.

Sin will constantly find new ways to appear and reside in our culture and our lives. Because sin is an ever-relevant problem, it should be ever addressed in the church. We do not cease to become sinners. Furthermore, the enemy of our souls longs for sin to grow and reside in our lives. He will hide sin in the media we consume. He will disguise sin in ways we do not recognize. He will inflate our pride and convince us that minor sins are trivial, and we need not worry about them. Satan works endlessly to drag the world and believers into sin, so the church and everyday Christians should never cease to fight against it.

More than being a reality of our present world, sin is also a prominent theme in the Bible. Sin's existence came from the fall of man. God brought about the fall of the Northern and Southern kingdoms of Israel because of their sin. God pronounced judgment on cities and nations for their grievous sins. Jesus died for the forgiveness of our sins. The reality of sin along with man's sinfulness finds its place all throughout the Bible. This is not to say that the Bible is a book of doom and gloom, only conveying the message that we are sinners. Rather, the Bible is a book that addresses reality, and sin is a prominent reality of our world. If it is such an undeniable reality, if the Bible speaks so often of sin and harshly condemns it, it would be proper for us to give the doctrine of sin its rightful place.

I believe that one of Satan's biggest goals is to make the church believe that sin and the doctrine of sin are no big deal. When the church disregards the ideas of sin and man's sinfulness as unimportant or even non-existent, sin is provided an environment in which it can flourish. If we are not acutely aware of sin, our sinfulness, and what God thinks about sin, we are likely to let it take root in our lives without even noticing. How many self-professing Christians lead lives full of sin and seem to believe there is no contradiction between their actions and their faith? How many "progressive Christians" deny the doctrine of sin, then go on to justify abominable and atrocious sexual acts? How often do we puff ourselves up with pride, thinking that we aren't really *that* sinful, only to let other sins run rampant in our lives as a result? Friends, Satan does not want us to believe in sin. He does not want God's judgment of sin proclaimed because wherever it is proclaimed, repentance and the salvation of souls follow. It would be entirely foolish of us to believe that presenting a sinless Christianity in order to draw in more converts and "cast a wider net" is actually God's will. Peter tells us God's will in his epistle: that He does not want "anyone to perish, but everyone to come to repentance" (2 Peter 3:9). One can only repent if they believe they have sins to repent of. It would be disingenuous and irrational for us to portray issues of sin and hell as a non-fundamental issue in order to appease the masses and create a falsified sense of unity. Sin is present in all our lives and is a key doctrine affirmed time and time again throughout Scripture. Let us not treat it as anything less.

Morally Bankrupt Culture

Due to the rampancy of sin and its widespread acceptance, the West is increasingly becoming a morally bankrupt culture. To echo an analogy made by Martin Luther King Jr., our culture writes a moral check that it has no way to pay and never had the intention of paying. This is not a self-righteous flashback about how "back in my day things were better." This is also not about stoking collective moral outrage over the smallest moral failures in society. This is a genuine analysis of the world we live in, and the moral bankruptcy that is ever prevalent.

To begin, moral relativism has taken over Western culture and the very concept of virtues and vices have been destroyed. Virtues and vices are defined by the individual, as we are encouraged to "live our truth" and do what "is right for us." A culture cannot claim to be moral yet laugh at the existence of absolute right and wrong. It appears as though the only virtues we do hold onto are those of pleasure and self-actualization. These are placed on a golden pedestal above things like truth, justice, and compassion. I do not believe this is an over exaggeration. The internet has turned the formerly shameful act of prostituting oneself into a viable career, and to decry this horrid abomination would be to self-righteously shame "sex workers." For some people, an 18-year-old posting explicit content online has the moral high ground over those who would condemn these actions. Gender and sexual identities have become so confusing and complicated, with people reinventing themselves on a daily basis, yet to question this process of self-actualization would impede on one's ability to "be true to themselves." Sexually promiscuous lifestyles have led to widespread STDs, broken up marriages, and destroyed our youth, yet culture claims that this is a natural part of embracing one's sexuality. Recreational marijuana usage has led to many addictions and stunted the motivation and drive of many, yet "stoner culture" is growing in popularity by the day.

Not only are pleasure and self-actualization the virtues above all others, but we fail to hold onto the few other values that we claim to champion. The people who "would do anything for their friends" will turn around and gossip about them. The champions of free speech and "speaking your truth" justify censorship against those whom they disagree with. The ones who march for justice will also commit injustice when it becomes beneficial to oneself, using past hurts as justification for enacting present evils. Those who champion women paving their own way disown those who choose to be stay-at-home moms. Our culture holds virtues selectively, when they are in one's self-interest.

Not only that, but evil is paraded and celebrated in the streets. The top music artists release songs with disgusting lyrical content which have been, in some cases, explicitly demonic. The most popular fiction authors of our day write books that are nothing more than a poorly written story used as cover for literary pornography. There are popular "dating" apps dedicated to doing nothing more than facilitating sexual encounters, these apps being downloaded nationwide. Millions of people march every year to support the "right" of one to dismember their child in the womb. One can only think of God's description of Judah when He says that "they have no shame at all; they do not even know how to blush" (Jeremiah 6:15).

In the midst of a culture that embraces and celebrates sin, who will stand up and speak a different message? Who will face the moral bankruptcy of the world and call it into account? Who will point out that society cannot live up to the standards it proclaims? Who will speak against the sinfulness of our nation and world, and direct these individuals with an eternal soul to a God who offers forgiveness? Is this too great a task? Is this too scary or difficult for people to do? Are there any who will follow the example of the biblical prophets and proclaim that we will be accountable to God?

Leonard Ravenhill, author and revivalist, writes in *Sodom Had No Bible* that "the average believer's complacency toward the lostness of men is appalling." I could not agree more. I have been appalled with my own complacency many times. When will the church speak up? When will Christians speak up? Do we not care about how sin is destroying those around us? People everywhere are suffering due to the consequences of sin left to run rampant. It tears apart families, destroys lives, and brings nothing but pain and ruin while whispering empty promises of pleasure. If we know that sin is this destructive, why do we not expose it? There are those in our lives who are being destroyed under the influence of alcohol, yet we are so terribly fearful of suggesting that alcohol abuse is sinful. There are marriages being destroyed due to sexual sin and pornography, but to call those people into repentance could bring uncomfortable conviction, and we would never want to make other people uncomfortable. It is pathetic that ministers and Christians today will watch sin absolutely tear apart the lives of their friends and loved ones, yet say nothing due to fear of "coming across too harsh."

Sin is very well leading to death in the lives of everyone around us, earthly and eternal. Will we name it as such? Will we let sin maintain a deathly stranglehold on others because we do not call people to turn from their sins and turn to Christ? Will we remain silent in order to preserve the comfort of others? Is that the legacy we want to leave? Are we willing to recount that to God at the end of our lives? "Yes, I saw how sin was actively harming all of those around me, but I really wanted to slowly draw people into the idea of Christianity, so while their lives fell apart I would slowly drop hints about God and faith." Of course, there is always discernment in how to bring up difficult truths, and sometimes the process takes a long time. Nevertheless, this does not excuse the complacency and inaction that have been present for far too long in the church. Jesus tells us that "You are the light of the world. A town built on a hill cannot be hidden. Neither do people light a lamp and put it under a bowl. Instead they put it on its stand, and it gives light to everyone in the house" (Matthew 5:14-15). What does light do? It expels darkness! It takes time for one's eyes to adjust to light. The light will seem harsh to those in darkness, yet many Christians believe that because of this, the light should be dimmed. Instead of truly being a light in the darkness of the world, Christians today have resolved to hide their light under a basket.

Conviction-less Preachers

In his masterpiece, *Why Revival Tarries*, Leonard Ravenhill writes that "this generation of preachers is responsible for this generation of sinners." As the common phrase says, "as the pulpit goes, so goes the church." Though Ravenhill's book was first published in 1959, those words still ring true today. Many Christians are sin-illiterate because many preachers are unwilling to address it. Because many Christians are sin-illiterate, they easily fall captive to sin. Oh, what sin do we see among professing Christians! Lifestyles and practices that would be foreign to unbelievers a century ago are common among believers today. All the while, as worldliness and sin infects the lives of believers, many preachers refuse to confront these issues. Some may say that preaching about sin is divisive, yet unaddressed sin is far more divisive because it separates us from God! Later in *Why Revival Tarries*, Ravenhill writes that "a preacher, however weighed down with degrees and doctorates, has not gotten far unless he knows soul-bitterness over the sin of this day." Preachers today take the pulpit unfazed by the sin of the world, and heartlessly indifferent toward the lostness of unrepentant sinners.

The solution to these problems is not to focus on everything besides sin. The solution is not to emphasize love while forgetting holiness. While the call to love our neighbor as ourselves is important and biblical, what has happened to the command to love God and to "be holy because I, the Lord your God, am holy" (Leviticus 19:2)? What the church needs is for preachers to echo Hosea's command, when he said, "Return, Israel, to the Lord your God. Your sins have been your downfall! Take words with you and return to the Lord. Say to him: 'Forgive all our sins and receive us graciously, that we may offer the fruit of our lips'" (Hosea 14:1-2). We need a genuine call to holiness. We need a reminder of God's hatred of sin. There is great darkness in the world, terrible evil that is horrendous to even speak of. When will the church shine the light on it? As church-goers flock to sin, some knowingly and some unknowingly, who will speak out that this is not what God wants for us? Christians everywhere are living in sin, and many of them do not even know that it is sin. Would the preachers of our day stand up and call the church to repentance and living a life of holiness!

No Grief Over Sin

Christians in our time have become accustomed to sin. We shrug our shoulders at what breaks the heart of God. What would previously have been moral outrage over the atrocities of the day have become weak or non-existent concern. If only we had a generation that was grieved over sin! If only we could emulate the example of Isaiah, when he says, "Woe to me … I am ruined! For I am a man of unclean lips, and I live among a people of unclean lips, and my eyes have seen the King, the Lord Almighty" (Isaiah 6:5). When encountering God, Isaiah felt great sorrow over his own sin and the sin of his nation. How many today would mock Isaiah for his sorrow, thinking he is making too big of a deal over sin, or that he has legalism entrenched in his heart? Friends, our hearts should break just the same as Isaiah's.

What would happen if we felt this same sorrow? How would our church change if we felt genuine sorrow over our sin? We scream for revival day and night, we claim to want a giant move of God, yet we never want God to convict us of our sin. We try to manufacture a revival without repentance, then stand confused when our world remains unmoved. Where are the Isaiahs of today? Where are those who understand the nature of sin, the holiness of God, and have a broken heart as a result? Maybe they have disappeared because talk about sin has disappeared from our churches, and our attitude toward sin is one of normalization. The younger generations live immersed in sin, to our dismay, yet their attitude toward sin is one they copy from us!

It is often said that the only thing needed for evil to triumph is for good men to sit back and do nothing. Similarly, the only thing needed for sin to flourish is for Godly men and women to sit back and say nothing. Only when our hearts break over sin will we be able to call others into repentance. We see that before Isaiah was called to do the work of God, his heart broke over sin. It was this deep understanding of his own sinfulness, as well as the world's, which pushed him into ministry. If only that attitude was a prerequisite to ministry today! How shameful is it that our ministers do not embody a deep desire for holiness in their congregations? It is tragic that the growing sinfulness of our world and congregations only causes us to shrug our shoulders and say "that's just how it is."

Faith heroes throughout history were always broken over the sin of their day. They were great men and women of God who saw the deep spiritual darkness in the world and strove to replace it with the light of the gospel. If only there would be more people whose hearts break for the sins of the world. Instead, contemporary Christianity looks down on those who have their hearts broken over sin. We view them as pessimists and tell them to look on the bright side. We call them legalists, madmen, or anything else to distract us from the fact that they are indeed right, and we have indeed let sin run unopposed. When people cry out against the thousands around them going to hell, we view their complaints as irrelevant because of the one person who came to Christ (though heaven does still rejoice over the one). When we mock those whose hearts are broken over sin, we mock the heart of God, which breaks far more over the sinfulness of this world than ours ever will.

Publicly denouncing sin and weeping over the fate of the lost does not signify an extremist position or legalist attitude. It is something Christ Himself does. When Jesus approached Jerusalem and "saw the city, he wept over it and said, 'If you, even you, had only known on this day what would bring you peace—but now it is hidden from your eyes'" (Luke 19:41-42). Jesus Himself wept over the fate of Jerusalem, the city that had rejected Christ and would face the terrible consequences as a result. Why did Christ weep? Because they rejected Himself, and "whoever rejects the Son will not see life, for God's wrath remains on them" (John 3:36). And why was God's wrath on them in the first place? Because of their sin! When people today weep over the lost and beg for sinners to be called to repentance, we write them off and say that they are focusing on such a small part of the Christian faith. When people today feel heartbroken over the sin of this current time, we mock them and say that they need to "loosen up a bit and stop taking everything so seriously." Oh, would our hearts change! Would our hearts reflect that of Christ Himself and of every man and woman of God who had changed the course of history.

A Rationalization of Sin

Worse than the fact that Christians today are not grieved over sin is the reality that many Christians today freely partake in sin. Christians listen to explicit music, watch TV shows full of sex, and frequently use words that I dare not repeat in this book. What is the justification often used? "It's not *that* bad." Christians today are so accustomed to sin that we naturally dismiss it. We know that TV shows will inevitably have profanity, but because of that, we unfortunately dismiss profanity as no big deal. We know that music will have suggestive lyrics, so we throw up our hands and say, "What else can you do?" Other times we may argue that the things we partake in "could be worse." This is not a good defense, rather an admission that the sin we partake in is justified because it is not as bad as other things. What a sad state the church is in. Much of the media found today is effectively debauchery with a cherry on top, and Christians flock toward it saying that "I'm only in it for the cherry." When taking a step back, it is almost comical how accustomed we have become toward sin. There are TV shows and movies that have explicit sex scenes. There are literally parts of the shows that graphically feature people having sex, and Christians will be relatively unphased. How shameful have we become! We would rather consume sin-saturated media than no media at all. And our reasoning in all of this is often that "it's not *that* bad."

What is even worse, is that when some Christians complain, the rest turn on them and tell them to grow up! Can you imagine that? We call people legalists for opposing sin-saturated media. If a Christian complains about explicit music, we tell them that they should lighten up. If a Christian refuses to watch a show with graphic content, we assume that they must have some type of inner sin struggle. Believers are no longer mortified over sin, and they laugh at those who are. I wonder what a most holy God is thinking when He sees Christians watching films containing graphic depictions of sex. What about when film characters use Christ's name as a curse word? Does God truly think, "Well, the rest of this movie is really entertaining, so the sinful aspects are no longer sinful?" Some today read pornographic literature by arguing it's just about the "compelling story," or listen to explicit music because they "are only in it for the good beat." Have we really used the inevitability of sin as a reason to justify partaking in it? Now, this does not mean that we adopt a retreatism mindset and abstain from anything containing even the slightest amount of sin. That would require us to leave this world altogether, because everything contains some amount of sin. I am not arguing that a movie with one scantily clad background character is unwatchable. Neither that a book with one swear word is unreadable. Rather, I am arguing that Christians should be aware of the content they consume, living obediently to Christ and making wise choices "because the days are evil" (Ephesians 5:16).

A retreatism mindset may be wrong, but the alternative is not to blindly accept everything. Sin is an unavoidable part of our world, yet that does not mean we should approve it when it appears. King David knew that it mattered what his eyes took in, saying that he "will not look with approval on anything that is vile" (Psalm 101:3). I pray more Christians would adopt that attitude. Christians are letting their minds, hearts, and souls become tainted and twisted by media whose sole appeal and goal is the romanticization of sin. Media today often throws sin in our faces while sending the message that it is good and exciting. Many movies and TV shows are just repackaged opportunities for voyeurism. Many video games are about the opportunity to commit evil actions, only virtually with no real world consequences. Does this mean nothing to Christians? While we are not called to abandon the world, can we at least abstain from the things of this world? Can we stop pretending that because we are Christians, we can fill our lives with sinful movies, shows, conversations, and music, and walk away unscathed? Are we magically immune to sin? Not at all! Let us not run toward sin under the premise of entertainment. It would be far better that we remain unentertained.

Sin Makes Sense of the World

For Christians and non-Christians alike, the doctrine of sin and the sinfulness of man is a necessity if we are ever to comprehend the world around us. It is no secret that the world is full of evil. When confronted with this evil, sometimes all we can do is ask "why?" Why do men violate women in their imaginations? Why do school shooters harm innocent children? Why do women rent out their bodies to the highest bidder? Why is domestic abuse a prevalent problem in the world? Why do pedophiles kidnap children to commit unspeakable atrocities? The only way to understand this, and I truly mean the only way, is with the doctrine of the sinfulness of man. The truth is not simply that human beings have a capacity for evil and wrongdoing, but we have a tendency and desire to do it. That is the only explanation that will ever make sense.

Many liberal theologians deny the sinful nature of man and choose to believe that humanity is inherently good while maintaining a capacity for wrongdoing. Yet, I cannot see how this mental framework leads to anything but nihilism. What is worse, assuming that human beings have an internal desire for evil and act upon it, or believing that humans are inherently good with no internal desire for evil yet still choose it? That would be a terrible belief to hold. How can anybody believe that a man with no internal draw towards evil would randomly decide to rape a woman? Are we to assume that those who consume child pornography have no evil nature? What about those who decide to shoot children in schools? Are we to believe that school shooters are inherently good? If you deny the doctrine of sin and man's internal sinfulness, there is no explanation for the evil of the world other than inherently good individuals choosing evil for the fun of it. If that is the problem, there is no hope and no solution.

Those who deny the sinfulness of man cannot find a meaningful explanation for the sin problem, because they do not admit that man has a problem to begin with. They will try to reduce the evil of the world to a long list of sociological, psychological, economic, and political reasons. One may try to explain how morally reprehensible actions are committed due to a variety of amoral circumstances, yet none of those explanations will truly suffice. While I do acknowledge that some people make poor decisions pressured by circumstances outside their control, the problem of evil cannot be solved by pointing outward. Blaming everything other than the individual may result in a minorly satisfying explanation, but it will never explain why so much evil occurs on a daily basis. Taking a look at the world, it is obvious that there is something wrong with mankind. There is indeed something wrong with mankind: sin. Luckily, there is hope to be found in Biblical Christianity. A biblical mindset would say that man has a sinful nature, that a draw towards evil is a part of the human condition. Biblical Christianity also offers a solution to this problem, the solution being found in the transformative work of God.

Not only does the doctrine of sin help us understand the world around us, but understanding my own sinfulness helps me make sense of myself. On many occasions I have resonated with Paul when he writes that "I do not understand what I do. For what I want to do I do not do, but what I hate I do" (Romans 7:15). Why do I do what I hate? What causes me to make mistakes and hurt those I love? Why do I do things I strive to avoid? The answer is sin. That is the only explanation. That is the only explanation for the internal struggle that everyone faces. I commit wrongdoing because my nature is inclined to commit wrongdoing. This is an explanation many Christians are uncomfortable with and try to deny. After all, it would seem cruel to tell others that they have a sinful nature.

Unfortunately, if we deny the sinfulness of man to protect the self-image of our listeners, we simultaneously set them up for self-loathing when they discover their sinful tendencies and have no suitable explanation. I can spend hours upon hours putting myself down, asking why I can't just "be better" and "not mess up", yet things make a lot more sense when I remember that I am a sinner. Because I know that I am a sinner, I have a hope in the finished work of the cross and the sanctifying work of the Holy Spirit. For those who do not believe in the sinfulness of man, they will be caught in an endless cycle of striving and self-loathing in which their best efforts continually fall short with no explanation as to why.

For those who acknowledge their sinfulness, there is hope in Christ. There is hope that the Holy Spirit will do a sanctifying work in their hearts and minds to conform them to the image of Christ. There is hope in the fact that there is a God who will take our heart of stone and replace it with a heart of flesh, that someone will do the work in us that we cannot do on our own. It would be foolish to keep this hope from anyone.

Conclusion

Sin is real, and it is everywhere. Sin is present in every aspect of our society, and it brings nothing but pain, death, and destruction through the allure of a temporary thrill. Sin is not simply the act of breaking one of the ten commandments, but it is a condition that all human beings have. In an increasingly sinful and morally bankrupt world, it is important that Christians speak openly and honestly about sin, not watering down discussions in order to hide a reality that may be harsh to others. Finally, without the doctrine of sin we cannot properly make sense of the world and ourselves, and we will have no hope when confronted with the evil that is present in the world and in our own hearts.

Chapter 2

Sin is Core to the Faith

Not only does the doctrine of sin make sense of the world, but the doctrines of sin and God's punishment of sin are core components of the Christian faith. They cannot be abandoned or forgotten. If they are, Christianity crumbles. While there are many who claim that these doctrines can simply be secondary issues or disputable doctrines, denying them or removing them from prominence means we must reevaluate and question everything else we know about Christianity. While the Christian faith is much more than the doctrines of sin, our own sinfulness, and hell, it is not less than that.

The Identity of Christ

I truly believe that if we are not honest about the reality of sin, if we hide this harsh truth behind layers of flowery language or ignore the topic all together, then we do a disservice to the person of Jesus. Without acknowledging the existence of sin and its eternal consequences, we risk losing Christ's identity as our savior. Christ is not a savior unless He saves us from something, and without identifying ourselves as sinners we cannot identify Him as our savior.

Christ's identity as savior, from our sin and its eternal consequences, is one that is present throughout the entire Bible. When John the Baptist encounters Christ for the first time, he declares "Look, the Lamb of God who takes away the sin of the world!" (John 1:29). Isaiah 53, one of the most well-known prophecies about Christ, says that "He was pierced for our transgressions, He was crushed for our iniquities; the punishment that brought us peace was on Him, and by His wounds we are healed." (Isaiah 53:5). These are not the only examples. The testimony of the Bible is that Jesus is our Savior, saving us from our sins. It is a core aspect of His identity and should not be forgotten or lost. To remove any attribute of Jesus would leave one with a false Christ.

It would be fatal to deny the deity of Christ, or His sinlessness, or the fact that He is loving. Similarly, it would be catastrophic to deny Christ as savior. Very few people would bluntly deny that Christ is our savior (though there are some who do). Nonetheless, you cannot have Christ as savior without humans as sinners in desperate need of forgiveness. Jesus is commonly referred to as our "Lord and Savior," yet having Christ as savior begs the question of what He saves us from. To deny our sinfulness and its consequences would mean there is nothing for Jesus to save us from. If people do not understand why they need saving, they will never be able to understand Christ's role as savior.

Furthermore, without a doctrinal foundation of sin and God's punishment of sin, the whole purpose of the cross is abolished. Liberal theologians throughout history have tried to explain the purpose of the cross without acknowledging our sin and its consequences. For some, the cross is a call to live more moral lives. For others, it is a cruel reminder of how the world hates the idea of loving others. In the perspective of some, the cross is about Jesus identifying with the lowly. This is what James Cone believes, as expressed in his book *The Cross and the Lynching Tree* when he writes that the gospel is "a story about God's presence in Jesus' solidarity with the oppressed, which led to his death on the cross." All of these alternative explanations are weak attempts to explain Christ's death and sacrifice as something other than an atoning death for the forgiveness of sin. Not only that, but these "alternate cross theories" ignore all the places in Scripture where the death of Jesus is explicitly tied to forgiveness of sins. We know that "He is the atoning sacrifice for our sins, and not only for ours but also for the sins of the whole world" (1 John 2:2). Peter says that "'He himself bore our sins' in his body on the cross, so that we might die to sins and live for righteousness; 'by his wounds you have been healed'" (1 Peter 2:24). Without believing in sin and hell, these verses are meaningless. Christ is no longer a savior, and the cross becomes a tragedy instead of a victory.

Sin and the Gospel

Additionally, without belief in sin and hell, the gospel ceases to be the gospel. The gospel forms the very core of Christianity. To lose the gospel would cause one to lose the faith altogether. Without the bad news of sin, the good news loses all of what makes it good. The power of the gospel is held in the fact that it is the "power of God that brings salvation to everyone who believes" (Romans 1:16). What is this salvation from? Death and the judgment of God owed to us for our sins. The urgency of the gospel is held in the fact that "the wages of sin is death" (Romans 6:23). Our sin brings death, so we need to be saved from that death. The universal need of the gospel is held in the fact that "all have sinned and fall short of the glory of God" (Romans 3:23). Everybody sins, so everybody needs salvation. If the doctrines of sin and hell are removed from the faith, the gospel loses its power, urgency, and universal need. It ceases to be the gospel.

The gospel is the power of God for salvation. What are we being saved from? The eternal wrath of God due to us for our sins. That is what makes it the good news! It is good news because of what we have avoided, and the eternal life we can look forward to. Without acknowledging sin, and the punishment we deserve from God, what is the good news? There is none. Those who want to alter the true gospel by removing doctrines of sin and hell are left with pitiful replacements. "The gospel is that we love God and love others." "The gospel is that you are loved." "The gospel is that God wants to make the world a better place."

Not only are these false gospels, but none of them contain any power. None of them explain the spread of Christianity. None of them explain why martyrs die every day for the faith. None of them explain why missionaries risk their lives daily. Why are those in China tortured every day for the Christian faith? Is it because they believe that God wants to improve the world? Are missionaries in Islamic countries beheaded for telling others "God loves you?" Paul writes that "three times I was beaten with rods, once I was pelted with stones, three times I was shipwrecked, I spent a night and a day in the open sea" (2 Corinthians 11:25). Did he do all that to tell people to love God and their neighbor? Obviously not. Those messages, while not inherently bad, are not the real gospel. People everywhere are willing to give their lives for the true gospel, because they know that it is the best news anyone could ever receive. People everyday risk their earthly lives in order to guide others to the One who can provide eternal life.

Secondly, without acknowledging sin, the gospel loses any urgency it has. Why do we spread the gospel? Why do we call people to come to Christ? Because we know their fate without God. We know that without His grace, they face God's punishment for their sins. The driving force behind us sharing the gospel is the eternal fate of every individual. We are not preaching a good moral code, or inviting others to join our social movement, or giving people ideas to ponder. We are telling them about God who came down as a man and died as an atoning sacrifice for our sins. If we minimize the sinfulness of man, and some have gone so far as to deny it, then we lose any urgency to spread the gospel. Many false churches that claim the title Christian refuse to evangelize. I can guarantee that all these churches deny the punishment due to men for their sins.

If they do not believe that "the wages of sin is death" (Romans 6:23), why would they guide people to life? If Christ does not offer a forgiveness that everyone needs, why should anyone else become a Christian? If sin's only consequence is that it makes the world a worse place, then we should just preach self-improvement and moral living. If there is no such thing as hell, we should focus on making the world better and undoing sin, not preaching the gospel. As Christians, we spread the gospel because sin does much more than make the world a worse place. It leads to eternal death. The gospel has no urgency if we do not believe the eternal need for all to hear, and we cannot believe people truly need grace without believing in sin and hell.

Finally, the universal need of the gospel is rooted in the universality of sin. We know that "all have sinned and fall short of the glory of God" (Romans 3:23). Because all sin, all are in need of grace. As we have seen earlier, if we do not believe that sin is inherent to the human condition, why should we speak out against it? The church is filled with many who view sin as something outside of oneself. It is present in the world, in institutions or places of power, but never inside of people. So many churches are devoid of the gospel because they do not acknowledge the sinfulness of man. So many churches today are nothing more than social justice organization centers in which the injustices of the world are called out but never the sinfulness of our own hearts. These churches preach a message of behavioral modification, but never inward transformation by the Holy Spirit, because to preach this transformation would be to admit the sin that lives inside of us all. Friends, institutions are sinful because we are sinful. Governments are sinful because we are sinful. It is not abstract power structures that need saving, but us. Individuals are sinners. Individuals need Christ. Every person sins, and because every person sins they face the eternal wrath of God. This is why the gospel is universal, because sin is universal. To deny the universality of sin would be to deny the universal need of the gospel.

As we see, one cannot have the gospel without forgiveness of sin. Therefore, one cannot proclaim the gospel without proclaiming forgiveness of sin, and one cannot proclaim forgiveness of sin without proclaiming humanity to be sinful. We also cannot proclaim the need for forgiveness without proclaiming the existence of hell. Otherwise there is no eternal need to be forgiven. The gospel is central to the entire Christian faith. It is impossible to argue that there is anything more central to the Christian faith than the death and resurrection of Jesus Christ for the forgiveness of sins.

Without the belief in sin and hell, the gospel ceases to be the gospel, and whenever the gospel is not made the center of the Christian faith, bad things shortly follow. Without the doctrine of eternal punishment of sin, the gospel no longer becomes an eternal gospel, but an earthly one. Liberation theology, the prosperity gospel, and more, are all consequences of when the Christian message loses its eternal stakes. When we remove the eternal relevance of the gospel, all we can focus on is the earthly benefits of the gospel, which would include things like helping others, bringing about justice, and loving your neighbor. The actions that result from believing the gospel becomes the whole point of Christianity. The results of the gospel *become* the gospel. A heavenly and eternal gospel will have earthly and temporal benefits. An earthly and temporal gospel will have hellish and eternal consequences.

A Defense of Hell

At this time, I would like to make a defense of the doctrine of hell. There will be some Christians who will affirm the reality of sin, and maybe even our sinful nature, yet deny the existence of God's eternal punishment for sin. The doctrine of hell is one that many Christians shy away from or outright deny. It is something people find uncomfortable, and understandably so.

It can initially be uncomfortable to believe that people will face the wrath of an all holy and almighty God for their sins, especially when they are people we care about. Yet, without the doctrine of hell, we must critically re-evaluate many things about God, who He is, the Bible, and more.

Let us begin with the idea that God is just. Because He is just, God cares about right and wrong. God does not look at the wrongdoing of this world, and just shrug His shoulders and resolve to say, "that's how it is." Instead, God cares greatly about what goes on in this world, and He despises the evil in the world. When Habakkuk writes about God, he says that "Your eyes are too pure to look on evil; You cannot tolerate wrongdoing" (Habakkuk 1:13). God cares more about right and wrong than anyone on Earth ever could, and that is a good thing. I don't think we would want it differently. We also know that God will punish sin. Paul tells us that "we must all appear before the judgment seat of Christ, so that each of us may receive what is due us for the things done while in the body, whether good or bad" (2 Corinthians 5:10). God will make sure every wrongdoing gets its proper punishment. In his book *12 Things God Can't Do*, Nick Tucker, Vicar of St Bartholomew's Edgbaston in Birmingham, writes that "this is why it's good news that God cannot bear to look [on sin]. God is so utterly, morally pure, so deeply committed to justice that it will 'roll on like a river' with 'righteousness like a never-failing stream' (Amos 5:24)."

It is good news that God cares about sin and enacting justice. It would be terrible news if He didn't! Imagine a God who was indifferent to the Holocaust, indifferent to rape and murder, and didn't bat an eye when innocent civilians are killed by tyrannical governments. It is a good thing that God will punish sin to its fullest extent. The question becomes: how will He do it? Without believing in hell, believing that after this life God will give people what their actions deserve, we are left with a big problem. Whenever evil wins in the world, that is the end of the story. Without the belief in hell, Hitler dies without God punishing him. Without believing in hell, those who brutally used slaves to build their own empire get to die in luxury. Without believing in hell, rapists who never get caught will never get the justice they deserve. Without believing in hell, the only proper feeling we can have is despair. How terrible is it to see the evil in the world, and believe in a God who will not bring about eternal justice? How horrific is it to see cruel tragedy after tragedy and not believe that God cares and will do something about it? At this point, we can see that it is in our best interest to believe in a God who cares about sin and will punish it in the life to come. To believe that God punishes sin in the life to come is to believe in hell. Not believing this, not believing in hell, would present us with quite a bleak alternative.

Yet, we are now faced with a problem. We rejoice that God will pay back every sin that has been committed, for anything else would make God unjust. Yet we also commit a lot of sins ourselves. We may write them off and go "they are minor sins, God won't really care." But if we were to truly think about it, we would realize that we have much more sin than we realize, and that God cares about sin much more than we may initially believe. Many people want to believe that God will punish all the "bad guys," yet the "good people" will get to walk free. It is an easy mindset to adopt if one wants to deny accountability for their own sins, while still believing that God will punish those who "really deserve it." Yet if this were to be the case, God would not in fact be just. We know that "God does not show favoritism" (Romans 2:11). God judges everyone the same. We may be angry at the wrongdoings of the world yet assume that God will not be angry at our own. We allow God the right to enact justice on everybody except ourselves. But this is not how justice works. For someone to be truly just and fair, they must judge everyone equally. If God will punish the wrongdoings of those who we think deserve it, then He will punish our wrong doings as well.

So, we will have to face God and receive His just punishment for sin, which we just previously established is a good thing. If that were not true, we would be left with an unfair and unjust God who doesn't care about the evils committed in the world. But this gives us an unpleasant reality: we will be punished as well. God will repay us with everything that our wrongdoings deserve. The judgment of God sounds quite terrifying.

This is where Christ comes in. Without believing that Christ took on the punishment that we deserve, then the cross makes no sense. Why would the king of the universe come down as a man and accept a terribly brutal fate of death on a cross, if it were not to take away that terribly brutal fate from us? Isaiah 53 lays this concept out clearly when prophesying about Christ, saying that "he was pierced for our transgressions, he was crushed for our iniquities; the punishment that brought us peace was on him, and by his wounds we are healed. We all, like sheep, have gone astray, each of us has turned to our own way; and the Lord has laid on him the iniquity of us all" (Isaiah 53:5-6). It is clear that

Christ took on the punishment we deserved. Without believing that God punishes sin, which would constitute a belief in hell, then Christ's death makes no sense. We would have to come up with some alternate explanation for His death, which would not only be void of scriptural support, but would need to explain away portions of Scripture which blatantly imply the opposite.

Adding on, the Bible itself is full of verses detailing the fact that God's wrath will be poured out on sin. Not only is God's wrath and punishment of sin logical, something we should in fact desire, and something that makes sense of the cross, but God's wrath upon those who sin is an undeniable doctrine when reading the Bible. We know that through Jesus "we shall be saved from God's wrath" (Romans 5:9). In the Gospel of John, Jesus tells us that "Whoever believes in the Son has eternal life, but whoever rejects the Son will not see life, for God's wrath remains on them" (John 3:36). 2nd Thessalonians tells us that God "will punish those who do not know God and do not obey the gospel of our Lord Jesus. They will be punished with everlasting destruction and shut out from the presence of the Lord and from the glory of his might" (2 Thessalonians 1:8-9). I could list endless other verses that all demonstrate the truth that God hates sin and will pour out wrath upon sinners. God's eternal wrath on sin, which we call hell, is an undeniable Scriptural reality. To deny the existence of hell would be to ignore large portions of Scripture, and many of Christ's own words.

There are many who will counter my claims and argue that the idea of hell is a modern idea, that people did not start believing in hell until very recently. They may say that

Christians did not interpret the Bible that way until the last few centuries. Not only does this claim ignore the fact that God's wrath on sin is laid out plainly and clearly in Scripture but claims like these ignore history. It is clear that throughout church history, Christians believed in the eternal punishment of God for sin. Clement of Rome (AD 35-99) wrote that "those who have sinned and who have denied Jesus by their words or by their deeds are punished with terrible torture in unquenchable fire" (Second Clement 17:7). Polycarp (AD 69-155) wrote that "fixing their minds on the grace of Christ, [the martyrs] despised worldly tortures and purchased eternal life with but a single hour. To them, the fire of their cruel torturers was cold. They kept before their eyes their escape from the eternal and unquenchable fire" (Martyrdom of Polycarp 2:3).

Irenaeus (AD 130-202) said that "the penalty increases for those who do not believe the Word of God and despise his coming ... It is not merely temporal, but eternal. To whomsoever the Lord shall say, 'Depart from me, accursed ones, into the everlasting fire,' they will be damned forever" (Against Heresies 4:28:2). Cyril of Jerusalem (AD 313-386) wrote that "We shall be raised therefore, all with our bodies eternal, but not all with bodies alike: for if a man is righteous, he will receive a heavenly body, that he may be able worthily to hold converse with angels; but if a man is a sinner, he shall receive an eternal body, fitted to endure the penalties of sins, that he may burn eternally in fire, nor ever be consumed" (Catechetical Lectures 18:19). It is clear that hell is not a modern idea, but a belief that has been present since the beginning of church history. The doctrine that God will eternally punish sinners is not only logically consistent, but supported through examining God's character, through

Scripture, through Christ's death on the cross, and the writings of early Christians as well.

Old vs New Testament

Even though the existence of a God's eternal wrath on sin is evident, Christians can easily compartmentalize God into two parts, one of wrath and another of love. They may view the wrath of God as a thing of the past, while the love of God is our present reality. A common sentiment that many Christians have is that the Old Testament God is all anger and wrath while the New Testament God is all love and forgiveness. Some may ignore the anger and wrath of God, believing they are Old Testament characteristics made irrelevant by the coming of Christ in the New Testament. This is a logical fallacy, though, because it is founded on the idea that God somehow magically changed between the Old and New Testament. The idea that God changes is utterly false. In Malachi we read that "I the Lord do not change" (Malachi 3:6), and Hebrews tells us that "Jesus Christ is the same yesterday and today and forever" (Hebrews 13:8).

All the attributes of God found in the Old Testament carry over into the New, and anything that is true of God in the New Testament is also true of God in the Old. This sharp separation between a harsh Old Testament God and loving New Testament God is one that does not have a scriptural basis. In the Old Testament, time and time again, we see examples of God's love and mercy. Forgiveness and love are a common presiding theme of the Old Testament, as God remains patient with Israel in their sinful ways and does not abandon His covenant with them. In fact, if we want to see the harshest demonstration of God's anger and hatred toward sin, look no further than the New Testament. In the New Testament, we are able to see the fullest picture of God's wrath upon sin through the cross, in which God the Father sentenced the innocent and blameless God the Son to take on the punishment that we deserve. The song *In Christ Alone* echoes this truth in its lyrics, for "on that cross, as Jesus died, the wrath of God was satisfied." If we are squeamish at the idea of God punishing sin, then we must look away from the cross altogether. The cross in the ultimate punishment for sin, taken on by Christ who was sinless. If anyone wants to say that the New Testament God did not express His anger and wrath towards sin, the crucifixion of Christ proves that idea to be false.

This mental separation of an Old Testament God and New Testament God is simply a poorly constructed diversion in order to deny uncomfortable truths. To say "God is not like this anymore" is undeniably false and demonstrates a poor understanding of Scripture and who God is. Separating God into "two versions" is not just a modern trend but was found at the core of one of the early church heresies. Marcionism was a heretical belief pushed by a man named Marcion. When reading the Scriptures, Marcion felt that the Jesus of the New Testament could not be related to the "angry and wrathful" God of the Old Testament. To reconcile this tension, he proposed that the New Testament God who sent Christ is actually a different being than the God who created the world in the Old Testament. Needless to say, this belief was quickly condemned in the church. Mock it as we may, there are many Christians today who partake in mental-Marcionism, quietly separating the Old Testament and New Testament in their head and resolving that God as found in the Old Testament is irrelevant; that we only need to focus on God as revealed in the New Testament. It would be best to avoid this tragic error.

Even "Love" Books Talk About Sin

While we may not fall into blatant Marcionism, we may still view the Bible in a similar dualistic sense. Some Christians can easily come under the impression that certain parts of the Bible are sin focused, while others are love focused. Books like Romans are harsh and heavy on sin, while books like James and 1st John have the "true" heart of Christianity, which is to love each other. Those who avoid or even outright deny the ideas of sin and hell will gravitate towards books like James and 1st John while skipping over others. They may adore verses like "mercy triumphs over judgment" (James 2:13), "whoever does not love does not know God, because God is love" (1 John 4:8), or "and over all these virtues put on love, which binds them together in perfect unity" (Colossians 3:14). For some people, their Bible is only composed of verses like these. It is definitely tempting to live in the parts of the Bible that focus on love and avoid the parts that mention sin and hell.

What many people ignore, though, is the sobering fact that the very books which emphasize love also emphasize sin as well! Just three verses before "mercy triumphs over judgment," we see that "whoever keeps the whole law and yet stumbles at just one point is guilty of breaking all of it" (James 2:10). A few chapters before "God is love," we learn that "if we claim to have fellowship with Him and yet walk in the darkness, we lie and do not live out the truth" (1 John 1:6), and that "if we confess our sins, He is faithful and just and will forgive us our sins and purify us from all unrighteousness" (1 John 1:9). A few verses before "love … binds them together in perfect unity," it is commanded that we "put to death, therefore, whatever belongs to your earthly nature: sexual immorality, impurity, lust, evil desires and greed, which is idolatry. Because of these, the wrath of God is coming" (Colossians 3:5-6). Just as the wrathful traits of God in the Old Testament are present in the New Testament, the harsher Christian doctrines about sin are found in the "nicer" New Testament books as well.

In similar fashion, the parts of the Bible we tend to label as more "sin heavy" are also abounding with ideas of love of grace. The same book that says "all have sinned and fall short of the glory of God" (Romans 3:23) also says that "God demonstrates his own love for us in this: while we were still sinners, Christ died for us" (Romans 5:8). The same book that warns us that "if we deliberately keep on sinning after we have received the knowledge of the truth, no sacrifice for sins is left, but only a fearful expectation of judgment and of raging fire that will consume the enemies of God" (Hebrews 10:26-27), also tells us that we can "approach God's throne of grace with confidence, so that we may receive mercy and find grace to help us in our time of need" (Hebrews 4:16). The more "love heavy" verses and the "sin and hell" verses are woven together throughout all of Scripture. God's redemption always comes with the knowledge of what we need to be redeemed from. God's love of what is good will always come with His dislike of what is bad. You cannot separate one from the other, and the Bible does not either.

God's Love

Many people who avoid talking about sin and hell do so out of a desire to emphasize God's love. After all, that will be one of the biggest critiques made against the arguments presented here. What about God's love? Aren't we getting rid of it by talking about sin and hell? Instead of making people feel bad about themselves, why don't we remind them that they are so loved? While it is important to emphasize the love that God has for us, to do this at the expense of being silent on sin would not only be wrong but would prevent people from truly understanding the love that God has for us. It may seem counterintuitive initially, but understanding our sinfulness is necessary in truly understanding God's love.

It is easy for us to love things that are lovely. It is easy to love a beautiful flower. It is easy to love a precious newborn infant. It is never difficult to love things that are easy to love. It becomes a lot more difficult, though, to love things that hurt us or push back against us. Your child may be easy to love as a kindergartener, but what about when they are a rebellious teenager? Loving your spouse when things are good is rarely a challenge, but what about showing that same love after a fight? This may be a challenge for us, but it is not for God. By understanding this, we find a truth that makes God's love quite extraordinary. He loves us not because we are easy to love or because we are inherently lovely, but because loving us is a core attribute of who He is. He loves us when we feel like we are on top of the world, and when we are at our lowest point. His love for us originates in Him, not in us. He gives us His love; we do not draw it out of Him. He loves us because that's who He is: a God who loves His creation.

It is unfortunate that for how powerful God's love is, many people are unable to fully understand it. Why is this? Because they still view the reason for God's love as their own loveliness. This mindset inhibits us from understanding the magnitude of God's love for us and it can easily cause us to question God's love when we feel at our lowest. The instant that we make God's love dependent on some temporal aspect of ourselves, that is the instant we open the door to believing that we have lost it. If God loves me because I read my Bible often, what happens when that habit fades? If God loves me because I actively serve my community, what if I stop? If God loves me because I am nice to everyone, does He still love me if I wake up on the wrong side of the bed and become snappy and harsh? It would be heartbreaking for an individual to believe they have lost God's love. What is the remedy for these feelings of despair?

Surprisingly, it is not by reassuring ourselves that we have amazing qualities that God would love. It is actually the opposite. We must realize our own sinfulness. We must realize that even though we are all made in the image of God, it is an image that has been marred by sin. It is important for all Christians to understand that God does not love us *because* of our good qualities, but *despite* our sinful qualities. This makes God's love all the more powerful and eternal. Ironically enough, it is by understanding our own sinfulness that we understand how much we are truly loved. Because of this, when pastors and those in spiritual leadership refuse to acknowledge our sinfulness, they simultaneously refuse to illuminate the extent of love that God has for us. In some ways, it is almost God-ordained that preaching a message exclusively of love leads to a terrible understanding of God's love and its amazing power. We know that "God demonstrates his own love for us in this: while we were still sinners, Christ died for us" (Romans 5:8). The greatest demonstration of God's love is when He died for His sinful creation, that we may be forgiven and have eternal life. Without understanding that we are sinners, this beautiful verse from Romans becomes much different. It becomes "God demonstrates his own love for us in this" with nothing to follow. Without a proper understanding of sin and our sinfulness, God's greatest demonstration of love becomes void. For those who truly want others to understand the depths of God's love for them, it will have to include an understanding of sin, God's punishment of sin, and their own sinfulness. Only then can we experience and understand the most powerful love the world has ever known.

Conclusion

As demonstrated, the doctrines of sin and hell are key components of the Christian faith. Without them, we undermine who Jesus is and what the cross represents. Not only that, but we strip the gospel message of any power, urgency, and universality it may have. While some Christians try to separate God into an angry Old Testament God and a loving New Testament God, it is extremely clear that both God's love and wrath are woven together throughout the entire Bible. Even books of the Bible we deem as "more loving" are filled with references to sin and God's wrath, as well as vice versa. Ironically enough, those who try to do away with or ignore our sinfulness and God's justice hurt the very thing they are trying to uplift: God's love. Only with a proper understanding of sin and our sin nature can we ever begin to understand God's amazing love for us. We need to talk about sin. We need to talk about hell. We cannot deny their realities or do away with them, because in the process we will tear apart Christ, the gospel, the Bible, and God's love.

Chapter 3
Conviction is Important

As human beings, and sinful ones at that, we have a desire to avoid conviction. It always hurts to be confronted with something we are doing wrong, or something we haven't been doing that we should be. There is always a sting that comes with conviction, and that sting is not fun. Our dislike of conviction is not solely because of the sting it brings. In the battle between spirit and flesh, our flesh will desire to indulge in sin and numb our conviction about it. As sinful people, we will have a desire to avoid conviction about the sin in our lives, and when sin is spoken on, that very necessary conviction is brought into our hearts.

Isn't Conviction God's Job?

In a recent discussion about the spiritual health of my generation, I brought up the need for more convicting messages from pastors and spiritual leaders. There are many in my generation struggling with or freely partaking in sin, so I felt that it may be wise for pastors to take a stronger stance against sin with a renewed emphasis on holy living and the need for transformation through the Spirit. When I brought this concern up, I was met with the question: "Is it the pastor's job to convict, or the Holy Spirit's?" This question provided me with somewhat of a Catch-22. If I said that it was the pastor's job, I would be denying the work of the Holy Spirit in convicting those in the world. Christ Himself says that "when [the Holy Spirit] comes, He will convict the world concerning sin and righteousness and judgment" (John 16:8 ESV). I couldn't deny that. If I said that conviction was the Holy Spirit's job, then my desire for convicting messages was nullified. The pastor could say whatever he wanted, as conviction was up to the Holy Spirit.

This Catch-22 I faced, though, could be easily resolved through examining the prophets in Scripture. The prophets were known for their harsh messages to Israel and the surrounding nations, strongly calling out their sin, iniquity, and perversion that had taken over their societies. Now, let me ask, were the prophets needed? Did they play a part in convicting Israel? Anybody would say yes. Did God help bring conviction to those who heard the words of the prophets? Did God play a part in convicting Israel? Anybody would say yes. Could the prophets say whatever they wanted and expect results? Could they water down their message and in good faith say that "it's up to God"? Obviously not. As we can see, the dichotomy of "the words spoken or the Holy Spirit" is a false one. The Holy Spirit does the work of conviction in the hearts of those in the world, often through the words that people speak. It would be foolish to assume that our words do not matter. Our word choices have consequences. If we want the Holy Spirit to move in powerful ways, convicting those in sin and having them turn to Christ, we must ask ourselves if the words we use are setting the stage or tearing it down.

Godly Sorrow

Many oppose preaching on sin by arguing that it will bring about sadness in those who listen. If we were to bring up sin as a topic in a sermon, if we were to ask the difficult questions, we would make others feel bad about themselves. We wouldn't want that, would we? Luckily, the Bible addresses this very issue. In his second letter to the Corinthians, Paul writes that "Godly sorrow brings repentance that leads to salvation and leaves no regret, but worldly sorrow brings death" (2 Corinthians 7:10). Paul is not opposing sorrow, but rather endorsing the right type of sorrow. Paul wanted people to feel sorrow, as long as it was the right type. Godly sorrow is not a bad thing. Conviction is not a bad thing. In fact, it is this very sorrow that draws people to repentance!

Throughout Scripture, those who repented would tear their clothes or wear sackcloth. They would mourn over their own sinful ways and beg God for mercy. Whenever people returned to God from their old ways, there was sadness over how they had been living. Our modern society would never dare let people feel this sadness. One of the most precious things to individuals is their self-image. Unfortunately, many preachers have entered the business of protecting this self-image at all costs. Any drop of sorrow, any sense of self-lacking, is drowned out in endless affirmations of God's love that lead to nothing more than pride and contentment with ungodly living.

The sorrow of our world brings death and despair, for no hope accompanies it. Worldly sorrow provides no means of restoration, no path of reconciliation. The only option is endlessly trying to "be better" and remove the wrongdoing in our lives by force. This will never work, for the flesh cannot beat the flesh. If I feel worldly sorrow, my only hope is to strive for self-improvement, yet I will never reach the end goal. I will still commit wrongdoing, feel sorrow yet again, and enter into hopelessness. The hopelessness that worldly sorrow brings leads many to either numb themselves to any sense of conviction, or wallow in an endless pool of self-loathing.

Neither option is good. The former leads people deeper into sin, while the latter can lead to self-destruction. Godly sorrow, on the other hand, brings conviction as well as hope. Godly sorrow points people back to a savior who can redeem them. Godly sorrow encourages holy living and provides the hope that God will help us live for Him. Godly sorrow is accompanied by the overwhelming love of God. Godly sorrow never exists for the sake of sorrow, but has a purpose. It leads us to repentance, and repentance leads us to joy! To experience the true joy that comes from the forgiveness of our sins, we must experience the Godly sorrow that comes with the conviction of our sins. What an amazing God we serve, who does not leave us in despair but uplifts us grace and fills us with His joy!

As much as people may desire to avoid Godly sorrow, it is the only way that we can truly experience the joy of redemption. We cannot have proper joy in our salvation, we cannot glory in the grace of our God, if that salvation and grace are not put into perspective. It would be like receiving a parking ticket and having it paid off by an anonymous donor. One would be happy about that, for sure. But, what if that parking ticket was for one billion dollars? To pay it off, one would need to sell all their possessions and take out massive loans. It would be an overwhelming and unpayable debt. If one knew the extent of what they owed, they would be much more joyful when their fine was paid. It is the same with Christianity. One cannot properly rejoice in their salvation unless that salvation is put into perspective. And salvation cannot be put into perspective without understanding our deep sinfulness, which would bring about Godly sorrow, yet sorrow nonetheless. Godly sorrow brings people to repentance, but many Christians avoid it like the plague. Many do not want to invoke any type of sorrow in non-believers, even if it is important. Scripture itself says that this sorrow would bring people to Christ, yet preserving one's temporal happiness is somehow more valuable than one's eternal soul. If only our society had Godly sorrow! If only our preaching brought this about in others! We are in need of someone who will stand and say that "you are a great sinner in need of a great savior," despite the negative feelings it may stir up. If God Himself encourages this godly sorrow, who are we to avoid it?

The Law is Good

One thing that brings about this necessary and Godly sorrow is the preaching of the law. When preaching the law, we show God's requirement for how we should live, and expose how we have fallen short of that. Knowing that we break God's law, and that we will be punished for it, will bring about Godly sorrow. Yet this sorrow will point us back to Christ. Many will believe that the preaching of the law of God is unnecessary, that we live in an era where preaching God's love is all that is needed. Paul seems to take a sharply different approach than this. We see that he finds the law to be extremely valuable. He says that "What shall we say, then? Is the law sinful? Certainly not! Nevertheless, I would not have known what sin was had it not been for the law" (Romans 7:7). For Paul, knowledge of the law was a good thing. Why? Because only by understanding their sinfulness can people ever truly come to the Savior, and understanding the law leads people to understand their sinfulness.

In *Christianity and Liberalism*, J. Gresham Machen, a 20th century New Testament theologian, writes that:

> "Although Christianity does not end with the broken heart, it does begin with the broken heart; it begins with the consciousness of sin. Without the consciousness of sin, the whole of the gospel will seem to be an idle tale. But how can the consciousness of sin be revived? Something no doubt can be accomplished by the proclamation of the law of God, for the law reveals transgressions. The whole of the law, moreover, should be proclaimed."

Only with consciousness of sin would the gospel ever be exciting to an individual. Though he lived a century ago, Machen faced problems in his time that were very similar to what we see today. Mainly, Christians in his era were hand-crafting their own version of Christianity that was more or less a vague conglomeration of self-righteousness, good works, and following moral examples. What the liberal Christians (liberal theologically, not politically) had done was remove the concept of sin from the faith and Christianity had become unrecognizable as a result. Furthermore, it made faith for those in these liberal churches quite stale. The gospel was an "idle tale" and had become boring.

For many Christian today, the gospel is an "idle tale." Faith is something that is boring. Christianity is not exciting. It is a faith where you check the boxes, do the right spiritual things, try to live a good life, and get a ticket to heaven at the end of it all. Youth students who may have been on fire for God become disenchanted when the hype and excitement are gone. College students who compare their "boring" faith to the enticing thrill of sin almost always choose the latter. Adults who think that faith is nothing more than a religious routine will eventually abandon the routine. People like these have not been gripped by the gospel. They have not been caught up in the marvelous story of the cross. Christianity has become boring, deemed an irrelevant facet of one's life. This could be changed if the law is preached, and people were truly conscious of their own sin.

First and foremost, true consciousness of sin would lead to a refreshing wave of repentance. This would be of great benefit to the individual, the church, and society at large. Secondly, true consciousness of sin would mean the gospel is no longer an idle tale. The gospel would become personal for so many more if they only understood the depth of their sin. When someone truly understands their sinfulness and their need for savior, the gospel is longer "Jesus died for sins." It becomes "Jesus died for *my* sins." What a powerful shift! Not only that, but Jesus is no longer perceived as a distant God, but the ever-close God who saved, saves, and will continue to save. He is the God who catches us when we fall, and who meets our sinfulness with love and forgiveness. He is the God who holds us fast and sanctifies us. What an exciting story to be caught up in! This understanding can only take root in the heart of an individual, though, if they understand their sinfulness and need for savior. Otherwise, Christ and the cross are bound to remain distant and uninteresting.

Though we may have a stigma against the law, Christ does not. We can tend to view Jesus as someone who came to "do away with the rules" and to create a new order of love, joy, and doing whatever you want. Jesus speaks to something much different. He tells us to "not think that I have come to abolish the Law or the Prophets; I have not come to abolish them but to fulfill them. For truly I tell you, until heaven and earth disappear, not the smallest letter, not the least stroke of a pen, will by any means disappear from the Law until everything is accomplished" (Matthew 5:17-18). Christ speaks of how He did not come to do away with the law but fulfill it, and that the law of God will remain forever. Christ's coming does not change the importance of God's moral law or its relevance. Right and wrong are still right and wrong, and we are still held accountable to God for our actions. Jesus' life was one that obeyed the law perfectly, and His death was one that paid the price for transgressing God's law. The moral commands of God are still relevant for us, even though the consequences of their transgression were paid through His sacrifice.

In no way did Christ do away with the law. Not only does Christ affirm God's moral standards for us, but Jesus called His followers to a much higher standard of living than they may initially believe they are held to. In the Sermon on the Mount, many times Jesus begins His sentences with "you have heard it said." He then follows this introduction by stating a requirement of the law. He follows that by saying "but I tell you." This is followed by a commandment that calls one's heart and mind into account, not just one's actions. It is not just enough to avoid committing adultery, but even looking at another person lustfully is a form of adultery. It is not just enough to love your neighbor, but you should love your enemy as well. While murder is wrong, holding onto unrighteous anger is just as bad. Christ does more than just acknowledge the importance of the law. He reveals the true requirements of it.

In that same sermon, Jesus also warns against ignoring the law. He says that "anyone who sets aside one of the least of these commands and teaches others accordingly will be called least in the kingdom of heaven" (Matthew 5:19). Jesus Himself encourages us to not ignore the law and speaks poorly of those who do. Aren't we guilty of ignoring the law today? How many well-meaning ministers and Christians ignore the fact that we are accountable to God in order to "draw people in"? How many people minimize the importance of God's commands and teach others to view them with little importance too? The church today is full of leaders who set aside commands regarding sexuality, the sanctity of life, holy living, and serving others, thinking that they are doing a service to the church by "casting a wide net" to make Christianity more appealing to others. If only they read Christ's words in Matthew 5!

King Josiah

One story I quite enjoy from the Bible is that of King Josiah. While he reigned, Judah was entrenched in pagan worship. They served the gods of the surrounding nations and lived lives full of immortality. Josiah's heart is eventually gripped by the law of God, though, and in 2nd Kings we see that:

> "Hilkiah the high priest said to Shaphan the secretary, 'I have found the Book of the Law in the temple of the Lord.' He gave it to Shaphan, who read it. Then Shaphan the secretary went to the king and reported to him: 'Your officials have paid out the money that was in the temple of the Lord and have entrusted it to the workers and supervisors at the temple.' Then Shaphan the secretary informed the king, 'Hilkiah the priest has given me a book.' And Shaphan read from it in the presence of the king. When the king heard the words of the Book of the Law, he tore his robes. He gave these orders to Hilkiah the priest, Ahikam son of Shaphan, Akbor son of Micaiah, Shaphan the secretary and Asaiah the king's attendant: 'Go and inquire of the Lord for me and for the people and for all Judah about what is written in this book that has been found. Great is the Lord's anger that burns against us because those who have gone before us have not obeyed the words of this book; they have not acted in accordance with all that is written there concerning us'" (2 Kings 22:8-13).

Josiah has no prior knowledge of the law and is brought face to face with the law of God. As a result, he is exposed to his own personal sin along with the sin of Judah. What was Josiah's response to this revealing of transgressions? "This is too harsh." "I wish it was phrased with different wording." "I don't want to feel bad about myself." Not at all! When his sin was revealed, Josiah tore his robe and repented. He not only turned his own life around but led a sweeping religious reform in the nation of Judah. He destroyed everything in Israel not dedicated to God, whether that be temples, altars, or false priests and prophets. The law of God had convicted him, and he responded appropriately. It was the knowledge of his sin that convicted Josiah and caused him to repent. Likewise, it is the knowledge of our sin that leads us to repentance and challenges us to follow Christ deeper. It is through genuine conviction that we understand where sin is present in our lives, and through the Holy Spirit, die to self to live for Christ.

If only the law were read in churches today. So much would change! Now, the law should never be read in a way that implies we can achieve righteousness through our own works. There are many instances throughout history, the Pharisees being a prominent example, in which an overemphasis of the law led to a misunderstanding of its purpose. A primary purpose of the law is not only to show us how to live, but to expose our sin. Paul writes that "I would not have known what sin was had it not been for the law" (Romans 7:7). When sin is exposed, the path to receive grace and forgiveness is paved. Christians today need to develop a healthy understanding of the law, which is always paired with grace. Law without grace breeds hopelessness, and grace without the law breeds lawlessness. When King Josiah rediscovered the law, he did not simply give up. His despair was paired with action. Why is that? Because while the law condemned many things that Israel was doing and detailed God's wrath on those who do such things, it also showed the way out: turning back to God. Even in the Old Testament, God's grace is prominent and ever evident. The law breaks us down, so we can receive the grace of God which lifts us back up. If only Christians today rediscovered the law. I pray that we have a healthy conviction of sin that causes us to throw ourselves at the foot of the cross. What would change in the hearts and minds of people today if we presented both God's law and grace, not excluding one or the other? Would there be more like Josiah in our age!

The Tax Collector and The Pharisee

Examples of healthy conviction are not just found in Old Testament kings, but in the New Testament as well. In the Gospel of Luke, Christ gives us a parable about a tax collector and a pharisee.

"Two men went up to the temple to pray, one a Pharisee and the other a tax collector. The Pharisee stood by himself and prayed: 'God, I thank you that I am not like other people—robbers, evildoers, adulterers—or even like this tax collector. I fast twice a week and give a tenth of all I get.' But the tax collector stood at a distance. He would not even look up to heaven, but beat his breast and said, 'God, have mercy on me, a sinner.' I tell you that this man, rather than the other, went home justified before God. For all those who exalt themselves will be humbled, and those who humble themselves will be exalted" (Luke 18:10-14).

What was the difference between these two? Why did one walk away justified while the other did not? What was the difference between the Pharisee and tax collector? Repentance and the knowledge of sin. The Pharisee had no understanding of his sin, choosing to boast rather than repent. The tax collector's knowledge of his sinfulness had pierced his heart. The Pharisee presented his works before God as a means of justification. The tax collector knew he had nothing to offer.

Without grievance over sin, we risk all becoming Pharisees. It could very well be that the modern church had bred a generation of Pharisees who are caught up in self-righteousness because the sinful nature of humanity was never exposed by the pulpit. If we do not properly address the issue of sin, the church will inevitably create the impression that righteousness can be obtained through trying our best to be obedient to the law. That was the trap of the Pharisees. They did all the "right things" yet at the same time were so far from God. It is quite ironic, how time and time again, even if their communities considered them to be the most righteous of anybody, the Pharisees as a whole were never the example of how to relate to God. The people who were made examples were the tax collectors, the prostitutes, and such. They were examples because of their repentance, not because of their works. Contrarily, the Pharisees encountered Christ's message of repentance and scoffed. After all, what did they have to repent of? They kept the law and did so many good works. Who was this man to say that they still fell short?

Is anyone in the modern church like that today? Are there those who believe that they have become good enough for heaven, who scoff at the proposition that they aren't? Are there those that believe they can obtain righteousness through their works? Pharisee-esque attitudes are bred when there is no humility. Humility is bred by understanding our need for Christ. Our need for Christ is bred through understanding our sinfulness. Without consistent reminder that we are saved on the basis of grace, we can unintentionally become those who boast in our works and pridefully look down on those who sin "more than we do." True repentance can only happen when there is true knowledge of sin. When we repent, we are not asking God to simply look over a few mistakes we made, a few "uh-ohs." We are asking God to forgive us and redeem us, knowing the only righteousness we could ever have is Christ's. Without true repentance, we cannot have true salvation. If Christ's parable is any indication, I believe we will be very surprised by who is in heaven. There will be a lot of "bad people" in heaven, and a lot of "good people" in hell. The difference will be knowledge of sin and genuine repentance.

Ironically, it is by not teaching sin and not explaining the inherent sinfulness of man that we create legalists and Pharisees. For all the talk about "avoiding the Pharisee mindset," avoiding the topic of sin creates those very people. Why is this? Well, when one truly understands their sinful nature, when they throw themselves at the foot of the cross for grace and forgiveness, they are far less likely to judge others in comparison to themselves. Why? Because they know that the only thing giving them right standing with God is Christ's imputed righteousness. What happens when we do not explain sin and the sinfulness of man? We run the risk of people believing that they are justified by their own works and actions. Instead of receiving grace and living differently as a result, Christianity becomes about doing all the right things and being in right standing with God as a result. After all, that is exactly what the Pharisees did. They looked at all the things they were doing, and how little everyone else was doing, and could do nothing other than say "thank you God that I'm not like that guy!" A proper understanding of his own sinfulness would have humbled the Pharisee very quickly.

Easy and Hard Messages to Speak

It is quite true that speaking about sin will never be popular. Conviction is not an overwhelmingly joyous feeling, despite how beneficial it is. This lack of popularity for those who speak the harsh truth is evident in the Old Testament. When preparing to go to war against a common enemy, the kings of Judah and Israel met. The king of Judah wanted to gain God's guidance in the matter and "asked, 'Is there no longer a prophet of the Lord here whom we can inquire of?' The king of Israel answered Jehoshaphat, 'There is still one prophet through whom we can inquire of the Lord, but I hate him because he never prophesies anything good about me, but always bad'" (1 Kings 22:7-8). The true prophet of the Lord only spoke the truth to the king of Israel, and for him the truth often included words of judgment. Because of this, the king of Israel worked his hardest to avoid this prophet. He even gives the reason, which was that this prophet "does not prophesy anything good regarding me."

Those who preach about sin today will receive a similar reaction. The classic phrase "if you have nothing nice to say, don't say it at all," has become the new law for many pastors and preachers. Being liked has become a litmus test for the effectiveness of one's ministry. Due to this, we never want to follow in the footsteps of the lone prophet, saying what needs to be said. If we dare be bold and want to feel like we are really "speaking the hard truth" (when we in fact are not), we often resort to "conviction" that is nothing more than gentle nudging. Many pastors are willing to challenge their congregations, but rarely in a way that could bring true conviction. Take for example, the exhortation that "it would be beneficial if we are kinder to others." The pastor's congregation thinks to themselves: "I could do a better job at kindness. I should work on that." This "conviction" was received easily, because it was phrased in the form of a good idea and habit that people should adopt. One could accept this idea without accepting that they have fallen short or sinned. While gentle encouragement for Christians has its proper use, one cannot say that gentle encouragement is the same as conviction.

Compare the previous message with a message that has a little more edge. "We are commanded in Scripture to love our neighbor as ourselves, and to care for the widow and the orphan. Christ Himself died out of love for us, and for many the job of loving our neighbor is relegated to the philanthropists and the charities. We should take seriously the call to love our neighbor as ourselves. We should treat it as a command to live out, rather than one simply to believe." This message may strike more at the hearts of the listener. It may cause an internal sting to be felt. It may cause the hearer to grumble that "I already do great, who is this preacher to suggest otherwise?" All the while, this message may also cause the hearers to deeply understand the call to love our neighbor as ourselves. When people speak the truth, however hard to hear, the Holy Spirit works at convicting the hearts and minds of the listeners.

Now, it would be improper for me to create a strawman argument and present the case that nobody ever speaks the word "sin" in church. There are many pastors and churches who believe that they are "tough on sin," but a more appropriate term would be "tough on some sins." If we genuinely examine the issues facing our culture, there are some sins that are much easier to talk about than others. Given the modern cultural landscape, it is not very difficult to talk about God's call to enact justice on Earth and to love our neighbor as ourselves. Issues of justice are ones that our world, especially my generation, is extremely passionate about. In the southern United States, it would not be difficult to talk about the sin of abortion. This does not mean that we should avoid speaking on abortion, or justice, or any other topic simply because our congregations are well versed on these issues. Rather, what many ministers do is speak repeatedly on the less convicting issues because of how it will be received by the congregation.

In the southern United States, it is quite easy to speak out against abortion. It is another thing to speak out against gossip. In the more politically liberal states, it is quite easy to stand as a Christian in favor of justice. It would be quite difficult to speak in favor of biblical sexual morality. (Believe me, I have tried.) Across the board, many Christians will often spend much more time focusing on what is easy to speak on and less convicting to hear in order to avoid saying what needs to be said. For example, I recently participated in a ministry where a major focus was "loving your neighbor." A majority of the messages were centered around or directly about Christ's call for us to love our neighbor. Now, speaking on this call is not an inherently bad thing. But this was the only call that was ever present. Those who partook in this ministry greatly struggled with sexual sin, alcohol abuse, and deceptive lies from false teachers, yet those topics were largely avoided. My heart broke. I saw those around me fall into sinful traps that this ministry had no plan of ever speaking on, and I witnessed the consequences of such behavior in real time.

Now, what may be even harder to talk about than sin is our sinful nature. Most people in the world do not mind admitting their mistakes. After all, no one would admit to being sinless. That's equivalent to claiming perfection. Talking about how we sin is a lot less challenging than talking about humanity's sinfulness. When admitting to sinning, people are only speaking to their actions, not to their identity. To admit being sinful, though, affects a person's identity. This is a much bigger deal. Throughout the Bible, the sinfulness of man is thematically and explicitly prevalent. Romans tells us that "there is no one righteous, not even one; there is no one who understands; there is no one who seeks God. All have turned away, they have together become worthless; there is no one who does good, not even one" (Romans 3:10-12). Likewise,

Proverbs asks us: "Who can say, 'I have kept my heart pure; I am clean and without sin'?" (Proverbs 20:9).

One core identity of man presented throughout Scripture is the inherent sinfulness of human beings. John even tells us that "if we claim to be without sin, we deceive ourselves and the truth is not in us" (1 John 1:8). The sin John is referring to here is not sin in relation to actions, but sinfulness as an attribute of humanity. In Mark, Jesus even attributes sinfulness to being a core human attribute, when He says that "it is from within, out of a person's heart, that evil thoughts come—sexual immorality, theft, murder, adultery, greed, malice, deceit, lewdness, envy, slander, arrogance and folly. All these evils come from inside and defile a person" (Mark 7:21-23). Jesus Himself says that humans are sinful and have evil inside of us.

To suggest that mankind is deeply sinful, in many modern Christians circles, would be treated as a form of heresy. How dare we suggest that there is something innately broken or flawed in human beings? Who would ever suggest that each person has an internal tendency and desire to do wrong? Denying the sinfulness of man is something becoming ever more popular in the western church. More theologically liberal churches and denominations are adopting the mindset that humans are not sinful, but simply commit acts of sin. A prominent example of this mindset is a book recently published entitled *The Diabolical Trinity: Healing Religious Trauma from a Wrathful God, Tormenting Hell, and a Sinful Self.* For the author, and those who endorsed the book, the idea of oneself being sinful is inherently trauma inducing and should be rejected. Many other books have been written on similar topics, in which inconsistent philosophy and out of context Bible verses are used to deny the truth of a sinful mankind.

It seems as though the root cause of denying man's sinfulness is pride. If the core problem of humanity is that we commit acts of sin, then all we need is behavioral modification. If the core problem of humanity is that we are sinful, that means we need a savior and internal transformation. This could very well explain why many churches deny man's sinfulness and God's punishment of sin: protecting our own pride and self-image. Unfortunately, this turns the Christian faith into nothing more than a call to help the world and do good. Without believing that we are sinners in need of a savior, how could Christianity be anything more? By denying the innate sinfulness of mankind and turning the Christian faith into a lifestyle of good works, one can save their own pride and boast in their own works.

Woman Caught in Adultery

Many people who deny truth of God's wrath on sin will often reference John 8, the story of the woman caught in adultery. In this story, there is a woman caught in the act of adultery who is brought out to be stoned. Jesus intercedes in the situation, telling the crowd that "any one of you who is without sin be the first to throw a stone at her" (John 8:7). One by one the men who came to stone her walk away. Once the men leave, Jesus tells the woman "I do not condemn you, either. Go. From now on do not sin any longer" (John 8:11 NASB). This passage is often used by those who desire to avoid bringing conviction upon others. They will look at a story like this and say, "Jesus didn't call out her sin, He only showed love." They then conclude that calling sinners to repentance in our gospel presentation is wrong. If Jesus didn't call this woman to repentance nor condemn her, we should follow suit and just love others. There are many things wrong with this line of thinking.

First, we must realize that the woman who committed adultery did in fact deserve punishment for her adultery. Mosaic law sentenced this woman to death for her actions. She was fully aware of this too. Because of that, when Jesus met with her, she was fully under the weight and guilt of sin. She did not need Jesus to reinforce that truth. Instead, the weight of her sin provided the perfect launching platform for the grace of God. In this story, Christ was not excusing sin nor showing that God will not punish it. Rather, He was exposing the hypocrisy of the Pharisees of who had also sinned before an all holy and almighty God. The Pharisees knew that the woman was under the judgment of God, but they ignored that the same was true of themselves. Furthermore, Jesus did not approve of the woman's sin, but told her to sin no more. He explicitly acknowledged that she had done something terribly wrong and called her to turn from her ways. Who could read that yet still believe God is permissive about sin?

This Bible passage reminds me of the wonderful book *The Cross and the Switchblade* by David Wilkerson, the founder of Teen Challenge, a faith-based drug recovery program. In his book, he chronicles how he traveled to New York and encountered kids and teenagers who were broken and harmed by shattered families, lives of meaningless sex, and terrible drug addiction. He introduced these people to the overwhelming love of Christ that transformed them and gave them new lives. It truly is a wonderful book that all believers should read, and I teared up multiple times when reading it. In his ministry, Wilkerson did not shy away from the truth about sin, yet he had no need to overexplain the consequences of sin. The teenagers on the New York streets were already broken by sin. Many of them were crushed under drug addiction, trapped in cycles of gang violence, or heartbroken over sexual encounters with quickly changing partners. If they already saw and felt the temporary consequences of their sin, Wilkerson could easily bring up sin's eternal consequences. They had already been "crushed under the law" in a sense, which meant that Christ's love and redemption through the cross was all the more readily accepted.

One thing that made Wilkerson's ministry so powerful was that those he encountered understood their own sinfulness. Many today who argue for a sin-less gospel or conviction-less messages forget that fewer and fewer people today are aware of their sinfulness. There are some genuine cases of those who think: "I am so broken as a person; I wish there was someone who could redeem me and transform me." When we do encounter people like this, we do not have to overexplain the truth about sin and God's punishment of sin. These people are already very aware of sin and how destructive it is. These people already have internalized that if they encounter God, they will have to account for their wrongdoings. We can lead our conversations by presenting God's love and grace because the foundation of sin and God's hatred of it has already been laid. There are still some of those people out there today, whether that be the alcoholic who is hurting, the porn addicted teenager full of shame, or the convicted felon rightfully afraid of the God he will face after death. For these people, we can give the greatest news ever in the grace of God, because they already know how much they need it.

Unfortunately, this attitude has become rarer and rarer as self-righteousness has become increasingly prevalent. The culture of hyper-self-love has taught people to believe that they are the kings and queens of the world, and to never for a second doubt their own goodness. Christians need to understand that we cannot introduce people to the grace of God until they are aware of their need for that grace. Some are already aware, but many are not. That is why the enemy rejoices when we remove sin and hell from our gospel presentations and pulpits. People will never cling to a savior they do not know they need. Forgiveness and repentance cannot be accepted if the sinner believes there is nothing to be forgiven of or sins to repent of. Grace is not grace unless the recipient knows that they need it. If we think that we earned it or deserved it, it is no longer grace. Paul tells us that when understanding our salvation, if it is "by grace, then it cannot be based on works; if it were, grace would no longer be grace" (Romans 11:6). In order to come to Jesus for grace, one must first know that they need grace!

There has been some debate and conversations over which order to present the gospel. Do we confront people with hell then introduce God's grace, or do we present God's grace as a rescue from hell? Either way, whether you lead with grace or hell, man's sinfulness and God's eternal punishment of sin will still be in the picture. That is a picture the enemy wants us to avoid at all costs. He rejoices over a hell-less gospel, over a

God who is all love but no justice, a heaven without a hell. Satan does not want us to convince people they are sinners in need of grace, for it is by this understanding that they are led to salvation.

Conclusion

Conviction is real, biblical, and very important. When convicted, we turn from our sinful ways and turn back to God. When we expose the sinfulness of men, when we confront them with how they've fallen short and how they face the punishment of God, godly sorrow is produced that leads to genuine repentance. The only way to bring about this conviction, to truly cause people to repent and trust in Christ, is through speaking on sin and God's punishment of it. We see this with King Josiah, with the tax collector, and with many others in Scripture who realized their deep need for God's mercy and grace. To avoid or deny doctrines of sin and hell, to intentionally avoid bringing about conviction, will have nothing other than catastrophic consequences.

Chapter 4

We Have a Responsibility

As Christians, we have a calling to share the gospel. Not only that, but we have a responsibility to communicate it well. To communicate it well means that we must fully explain it, which means we must address the topics of sin and hell. For those in ministry, as well as the layperson, we are called to tell others the good news about the grace and forgiveness to be found through the death and resurrection of Jesus Christ. We cannot properly fulfill our calling if we ignore the key and fundamental doctrines of sin and hell. Furthermore, we cannot lead others into deeper relationship with Christ unless we speak of sin which hinders that relationship.

Paul's Innocence

Paul was fully aware of this responsibility he carried. In his ministry, he knew that he must not avoid difficult topics or conversations, but boldly and faithfully proclaim the full truth. In his farewell remarks to the church in Ephesus, Paul says that "I declare to you today that I am innocent of the blood of any of you. For I have not hesitated to proclaim to you the whole will of God" (Acts 20:26-27). How many Christians could say that? How many pastors and preachers today could make the defense of Paul? When Paul traveled, he preached the entire gospel. He did not avoid the parts that were difficult to hear.

He did not change his message in order to make it appealing to others. Paul was innocent, preaching the truth without modification or revision. Nobody could accuse Paul of withholding vital information.

How many people today are innocent? How many refuse to mention sin, and as a result remove repentance from their message? Does our message include "the whole will of God"? Does our preaching exclude topics we find too uncomfortable to mention? Is our ministry bound by the Word and will of God, or is it merely influenced by it? In many ways we have stopped preaching the Word of God and turned to preaching specific words of God, words we often know will be well received. Paul knew that if his ministry were to randomly cease, no one could fault him for what he said or did not say. Just as it would be wrong to abandon speaking on sin and hell, it would also be wrong for anyone to exclude mention of God's love or His mercy or the transformative work of the Holy Spirit in our lives.

To intentionally exclude anything from what we preach would be harmful. Imagine if someone stopped speaking about the love of God. What would happen? They would be confronted by their congregation and those they shepherd. After all, they would be intentionally ignoring a major attribute of God, giving people an incomplete picture as a result. We would not give a pass for ignoring God's love, yet so many people today are given a pass when they ignore anything related to sin. It is a sad double standard. By ignoring doctrines of sin and hell, we are also presenting an incomplete picture of who God is. We are not proclaiming the whole will of God.

Jeremiah's Job

The prophet Jeremiah had no issue being honest and straightforward about Judah's sin and God's judgment. In fact, God Himself commanded Jeremiah to speak this way! God told Jeremiah to:

> "Stand in the courtyard of the Lord's house and speak to all the people of the towns of Judah who come to worship in the house of the Lord. Tell them everything I command you; do not omit a word. Perhaps they will listen and each will turn from their evil ways. Then I will relent and not inflict on them the disaster I was planning because of the evil they have done" (Jeremiah 26:2-3).

Notice, Jeremiah was told to not omit a word! He was to speak on Judah's evil deeds and the impending judgment they faced, fully and honestly. Jeremiah was tasked with speaking the truth, the whole truth, and nothing but the truth. To omit words would be to not only obscure the dire situation of Israel but to obscure God's message as well. How often do we omit words that must be said? How often do we revise what God has said because we believe that we can say it better than He has? Why have we become so utterly terrified to speak hard to hear truths? Are we so scared to hurt the pride of those around us that we avoid mentioning sin? Heroes of faith, both in the Bible and throughout history, were known for their strong messages of calling sinners to repentance. Today, we can't speak anything better than "Jesus wants to give you a big hug!" How pitiful we have become! We hide the gospel, the sinfulness of man, and hell, behind endless analogies and euphemisms so that others can't understand the truth because we ourselves would be uncomfortable explaining it!

Many church pastors and leaders model the false prophets found in the day of Jeremiah. When Jeremiah called people into repentance, because the destruction and wrath of God was drawing near, a multitude of voices quickly rose to drown him out. They proclaimed that Judah would not be destroyed, that it would not be harmed by a foreign empire. God proclaims judgment on these very prophets when He says "prophets and priests alike, all practice deceit. They dress the wound of my people as though it were not serious. 'Peace, peace,' they say, when there is no peace" (Jeremiah 6:13-14). These prophets were quick to soothe the ears of others and assure them that there was no real danger, that there would only ever be peace. This was extremely contrary to what God had said about Judah, and what He set into motion.

Pastors and preachers today endlessly speak "peace, peace" to the unrepentant sinner. Yet, for the unrepentant sinner, there is no peace. At my university, a pastor was invited to speak in our chapel services for an entire week. The phrase he repeated endlessly, and had the students repeat, was that "God's mind is made up about you and the news is good." While that is true for those who are saved, he failed to mention that for unrepentant sinners, God's mind is made up and the news is bad. There is everlasting punishment awaiting them for their sins. When there are those who rise up to speak this truth in the modern church, the chorus of "peace, peace" fights to be louder. Let us not deceive people and preach peace without pointing them to their only potential source of peace: the cross of Jesus Christ. Jeremiah's responsibility was to convey the Word of God and to not omit a word. Our calling is likewise.

Ezekiel's Call

We learn from Acts that our calling is to preach the whole counsel of God. We draw from Jeremiah that similar to his calling, we are also called to not omit any word. We learn more about our responsibility from the book of Ezekiel. As a prophet, Ezekiel was tasked with speaking on God's behalf to Israel, confronting them with their sinfulness and iniquity. In Ezekiel 33, Ezekiel receives a description of his responsibility, when told by God that:

> "I have made you a watchman for the people of Israel; so hear the word I speak and give them warning from me. When I say to the wicked, 'You wicked person, you will surely die,' and you do not speak out to dissuade them from their ways, that wicked person will die for their sin, and I will hold you accountable for their blood. But if you do warn the wicked person to turn from their ways and they do not do so, they will die for their sin, though you yourself will be saved" (Ezekiel 33:7-9).

This has been one of the most chilling passages in Scripture I have read in recent times. Ezekiel was told to be a watchman for the nation of Israel. Watchmen had the task of guarding the city and looking out for danger. If enemies were approaching, the watchman would sound the alarm to alert the city of the oncoming danger. If the watchman failed and did not alert the city when danger approached, his lack of action would lead to the untimely deaths of many. It was with this analogy that Ezekiel was given his charge. He was to warn Israel of their sin. God presented Ezekiel with a great responsibility. If he did not warn the people, and they died in their iniquity, God said that "I will hold you accountable for their blood." If he did warn the people, even if they did not listen, God told Ezekiel that he would be saved.

Likewise, we are called to be watchman and warn those around us. What is the greatest danger people face? Their sin and its eternal consequences! Even true Christians, though they may be saved, can still have their earthly lives brutally derailed by sin's effects. It is our job to warn. As our society crumbles into shambles of fornication, alcoholism, drug abuse, pornography, hatred, and the like, speeding down the road towards hell, many Christians can think of nothing better to do than endlessly cry "love your neighbor as yourself." As the city is laid siege from all sides, the watchmen can do nothing better than ensure that the roads are paved.

The watchmen of our age by and large are failing to provide a sufficient warning to those facing an eternity of hell. Many are self-prohibited from speaking the truth due to fear of failure and backlash they may face. Afraid that their warnings may fall on deaf ears, they conclude that it is better not to warn at all. Afraid of upsetting their listeners, they may decide to only speak nice things. Friends, when has success ever been a prerequisite to obedience? If the guarantee of success is a prerequisite for speaking up, every person should remain silent. Our silence does not prevent our failure, it only guarantees that we have no chance of success.

It is important to realize that God did not hold Ezekiel accountable to how many people turned back to God. Ezekiel was not responsible for guaranteeing the success of God's message. He was only accountable for his obedience. Likewise, God will hold us accountable for our obedience. God will hold us accountable to whether or not we spoke the truth, the whole truth, in love. That is our call, and that is what we must be obedient to. There will be many who say, "people won't listen if we give them the blunt truth. If it is too harsh, we might scare them away." Friends, there will always be discernment in how to best speak the truth of the gospel to those around us. There will always be discernment in how to call others into account before God. There will always be discernment over how to properly communicate the facts about hell and God's punishment of sin. Unfortunately, many people use this idea of discernment as a way to permanently stay "in the process of discerning" and never actually communicate anything. When faced with the task of communicating the truth, so many give up and decide to not communicate it at all.

Imagine if Ezekiel had done that. "I don't know if I will scare them away by speaking of destruction. Do you think that they will feel bad about themselves when I call out their sin?" What would Ezekiel do if he gave into these thoughts? He would likely have taken the route of hyper-safety and tried to gently nudge those around him into repentance. "Hey friends, I think we need to take a time of self-examination and check up on how we are living. It seems that God might be calling us into a season of pursuing justice to a greater extent." If any prophet of Scripture spoke like that, we would have read it. But none of them did. All of the prophets conveyed God's message as He relayed it to them, because they were not called to success but to obedience. Ezekiel was a watchman, and if he didn't properly warn, then blood would be on his hands. Likewise, we are called to warn, and not only to warn, but to give a proper warning. Let us not be so scared over "how to properly warn without invoking fear or guilt," that though the enemy floods the city, we fail to warn at all.

Sin and Cigarettes

I recently encountered a video that illustrated the truth of our responsibility well, created by pastor and popular Youtuber, Mike Winger. He compared mentioning hell to mentioning cancer when talking about smoking. When trying to convince someone to quit smoking, one could bring up many benefits of quitting. Your breath will be better. It is good for your teeth. It is much more socially acceptable. Imagine elaborating on those benefits, yet refusing to mention how smoking can lead to cancer because you do not want to spark fear in the smoker. That would be irresponsible. By refusing to mention lung cancer, one is intentionally disingenuous about the dangers of smoking, greatly reducing the chances that anyone quits.

Now compare tiptoeing around lung cancer to how many Christians tiptoe around sin and hell. We want to talk about all the benefits of coming to Christ, except our salvation from God's wrath. We speak of the joy of Christ. We speak of the great embrace found in God's love for us. We speak of the community to be found in the local church. Those are all amazing truths, yet we cannot speak these yet avoid speaking on sin and hell. By intentionally modifying our presentation of the Christian faith, we are disingenuous about what we believe. Not only that, but we hinder our own work of evangelism. If we are not honest and genuine about the realities of sin and hell, people will have less reason to come to Christ.

Returning to the previous example, what would happen if anti-smoking messaging refused to mention the risk of lung cancer? Many more people would have continued to smoke. Many of those people would have developed lung cancer and died. In many ways, the anti-smoking commercial companies would have been responsible for their intentionally incomplete message. If the smokers continued to smoke, knowing the risk of lung cancer, that would be their own fault. If the commercials didn't mention cancer, what are the commercial companies supposed to say? "I guess they didn't care enough about their teeth." "If only they cared more about the social implications." "I guess bad breath was acceptable to them." We would not blame the smoker in this instance. Rather, we would say of the commercial companies: "they did not care enough about the smoker to warn them."

Similarly, by erasing sin and hell from our evangelism and presentation of the gospel, we present a false picture of Christianity and hinder our own work of evangelism. What will we say? "I guess they did not want to experience the newness of life in Christ." "I guess Christian community was not enticing enough." How many more people would come to Jesus if we were honest about sin? Are we that numb to their eternal fates that we will ignore their destiny without Jesus? As Christians, our responsibility is not just to God and those in the church, but to those who are unsaved around us. We have a calling to spread the gospel to the sinner and give good news to the brokenhearted. I hope people will not look back and say of us: "they did not care enough about the sinner to warn them."

Charlie Peace

Even non-believers have noticed the apathy of Christians towards the lostness of men. In the 1800's there was a murderer in England by the name of Charlie Peace. Sentenced to death, he was on his "death walk" with the prison chaplain who was reading nonchalantly about hell from *The Consolations of Religion*. Shocked by his easy-going attitude about the subject, Peace confronted the chaplain and said:

> "Sir, if I believed what you and the church of God say that you believe, even if England were covered with broken glass from coast to coast, I would walk over it, if need be, on hands and knees and think it worthwhile living, just to save one soul from an eternal hell like that!"

Did the chaplain truly believe what he was reading aloud? And if he did believe it, did it really grip his heart and soul? Friends, do we really believe what we say about sin? Do we truly believe that it destroys lives? Do we truly understand how sin twists God's good design into something evil? Do we really believe that sinners face the eternal judgment of God for their sins? Do we understand the unspeakable eternity that is only a heartbeat away from many of our friends and family? Can we declare with confidence that the world is full of sin? If we do truly believe all these things, then why is there any hesitation to talk about it? If sin is the world's greatest problem, why do we leave it unaddressed in the pulpit and in our own conversations? We must either not believe the biblical realities about sin, or our heart has become calloused to how dastardly it truly is!

What would happen if the dead could talk to us? What would happen if the souls of those who had died and gone to hell could come back and speak with us? What would they say? Some may say "if you had only told me about hell, I would have repented." "If you had only told me of the terrible fate that awaited me, I would have come to Christ and clung to Him as my savior." "How could you claim to love me yet withhold this information from me?" If the dead could talk to us, I predict that we may hear some of these very things. The last question any of us want to ask ourselves is: what if I had mentioned hell? For ministers and church leaders nationwide, who refuse to address the sin of their flock and refuse to call sinners to repentance, some of their congregation will inevitably die without repenting and trusting Christ as savior. At that moment, all they will be left thinking is: "would things have gone differently if I told them the truth?"

Now, there are some who believe that all that is necessary is to bring up hell once and we have done our part. If we mention it once, then we have nothing more to do. In a conversation with some friends, I brought up the need for someone to sit down and share the gospel with a mutual friend of ours. The response I received was along the lines of: "she grew up in church and heard that hell is real. I want to respect her free will and not cram anything down her throat. She already knows about it, so we don't need to tell her." What a calloused heart! It is a heart that even I am guilty of having at times. For our mutual friend, it was not as if we had pleaded with her to come to Christ, as if we had laid out the gospel and our concern for her eternal fate, yet she still said no. She simply had heard growing up that hell was real, and my peers decided this was enough, that for us to bring it up again would be "cramming it down her throat." Charles Spurgeon, the esteemed 19th century pastor and author, said that:

> "If sinners be damned, at least let them leap to Hell over our dead bodies. And if they perish, let them perish with our arms wrapped about their knees, imploring them to stay. If Hell must be filled, let it be filled in the teeth of our exertions, and let not one go unwarned and unprayed for."

I pray that this is our attitude, that we fight for the souls of those we care about, that we share the truth with genuine love and concern. Sometimes this takes a series of conversations, other times only one. And if the truth is rejected, I pray that we enter the battlefield of prayer for their souls. As pastor and author Paul Washer says: "if I cannot talk to a person about God, I talk to God about that person." Either way, let us not treat the eternal fate of others as a passing care, giving a half-hearted effort then saying that we have done all we could.

Do Not Despise Christ's Words

In addition to what has been covered previously, we are also presented with a sobering truth given to us from Christ Himself. In the Gospel of Mark, Jesus tells us that "if anyone is ashamed of me and my words in this adulterous and sinful generation, the Son of Man will be ashamed of them when He comes in His Father's glory with the holy angels" (Mark 8:38). When reading this, I was given chills by the phrase "my words." Many Christians claim to be boldly unashamed of Christ, yet shy away from His words. Jesus says many things that seem quite harsh. He does not shy away from explaining the depravity of mankind, saying that "it is from within, out of a person's heart, that evil thoughts come—sexual immorality, theft, murder, adultery, greed, malice, deceit, lewdness, envy, slander, arrogance and folly" (Mark 7:21-22). He says that for those who would cause the little ones to stumble, it "would be better for them if a large millstone were hung around their neck and they were thrown into the sea" (Mark 9:42). Shortly after, Jesus mentions hell three times in a row, one of the times describing it as the place "where the fire never goes out" (Mark 9:43). The Gospel of Matthew records a scathing remark from Jesus, when He calls some people a "brood of vipers" (Matthew 12:34).

Many people are ashamed of these words that came from Jesus. Many people wish they could remove these words of His and become apologetic while explaining these things to others. "I know this seems bad, but trust me, Jesus is a great guy." Modern Christians often make excuses for what Jesus said and try to downplay His words. When Jesus says that "unless you repent, you too will all perish" (Luke 13:5), we explain that He is actually referring to the fact that if you do not change your ways and love your neighbor better, you will perish in an earthy sense. When Jesus says that the "Son of Man will send out His angels, and they will weed out of His kingdom everything that causes sin and all who do evil. They will throw them into the blazing furnace, where there will be weeping and gnashing of teeth" (Matthew 13:41-42), we make up some poorly composed, philosophical sounding argument that somehow explains the passage in a way that ignores its clear meaning. When Christ talks about salvation, and how for those not on the narrow path "there will be weeping there, and gnashing of teeth, when you see Abraham, Isaac and Jacob and all the prophets in the kingdom of God, but you yourselves thrown out" (Luke 13:28), we will do anything other than realize that Christ spoke of the eternal separation from God and the punishment that unrepentant sinners will face.

Very plainly, Jesus called sinners to repentance, exposed the great sinfulness of man, and mentioned hell multiple times throughout Scripture. To not stand by these statements would be to not stand by Jesus. It becomes all too clear why Jesus makes a connection between being ashamed of His words and being ashamed of Him. We cannot believe in Jesus without also believing what He said. We cannot claim to spread the words of Christ without spreading the words that make others uncomfortable. We have become all too ashamed of certain things that Jesus said, and He gives us a very dire warning of what will happen to those who are ashamed of His words.

So many Christians today are ashamed of the Jesus of the Bible. Many are much more comfortable with the Jesus they create in their heads. The Jesus of our minds often resembles a hippie who is fun, caring, and just wants to make sure that we love each other. That is the Jesus that many people follow. That is the Jesus that many churches preach on Sunday. That is why, when you look at churches who preach this "happy-fun-times" Christ, they will intentionally avoid any passage of Scripture that could compromise this image. They will avoid the high moral standards Christ presents. They will avoid places He talks about the judgment and wrath of God. They will avoid passages that present the truth of penal substitutionary atonement. It is passages like these that destroy the idol of hippie Jesus that many have set up. Christians follow this idol because they are ashamed and in denial of the true Christ as presented in Scripture.

In our Christian walk, we need to understand all aspects of Jesus. We need to see the Jesus that calls us to "love the Lord your God with all your heart and with all your soul and with all your mind and with all your strength" and to "love your neighbor as yourself" (Mark 12:30-31). We also need to see the Jesus that says: "Do you think I came to bring peace on earth? No, I tell you, but division" (Luke 12:51). We need the Jesus who tells the woman at the well: "neither do I condemn you" (John 8:11), as well as the Jesus that tells the Pharisees: "you snakes! You brood of vipers! How will you escape being condemned to hell?" (Matthew 23:33). We need to see the full and complete picture of Christ and who He is. If we intentionally exclude certain parts from the picture, if we are ashamed of Christ and His words, then we are following an idol and would do well to reread the warning He gives us in Mark 8. To avoid doctrines of sin and hell, to abandon or be ashamed of the words of our Lord and Savior, would be to abandon Him. To water His words down, to change them to fit the "culture of the day," would be to abandon His words and reject our responsibility to communicate His words and communicate them well.

Conclusion

We have a calling. We have a responsibility. It is not enough to believe in sin and hell but keep those doctrines in our back pocket to eventually be forgotten about or written off as irrelevant. We are called to convey the whole will of God, which includes sin and hell. We are called to not omit any of God's words, meaning that we cannot present a God who doesn't punish sin. We are called to be watchmen, warning the sinners around us of their fate without Christ. If we care about the sinner and their eternal fate, then we will tell them the hard truth. Finally, we see the sobering reality that to intentionally abandon the doctrines of sin and hell, to tuck them away from the light of day, would mean that we are ashamed of Christ and His very own words.

Chapter 5

The Consequences Are Real

Some may argue that I am being overly critical of the church. It may seem like I am making a big deal out of something seemingly minor. Friends, eternity is a big deal. The question of eternity is the most important question for every single person on the planet. I do not believe that we could take it too seriously. The doctrines of sin and hell are so important to the Christian faith that to abandon them would cause unknowing sinners to happily walk through the gates of hell and would set up the church for catastrophic failure in the future. The issues of sin and hell, and whether or not we actually speak on them, are very much a matter of eternal life and eternal death. For that reason, we must not water down these realities.

For many in the western church, language surrounding sin and sinfulness is something to be avoided. There is a desire to tone down the words we use. Instead of calling something sin, we use the phrase "ways we fall short." Instead of mentioning our sinfulness, we may say "brokenness" or "incompleteness." Instead of saying that Christ died for our sins, we will say that His "death brought life and restoration to our souls." While these statements may be true, they are often used to obscure the hard-to-hear truth. We must not hide key doctrines behind euphemisms and nice sounding words, hiding their meaning behind a false veil of friendliness. People must truly understand their sinfulness and need for a savior, otherwise their eternity is at stake.

Planes and Parachutes

In his book *The Way of the Master*, Ray Comfort identifies the consequences of ignoring realities about sin and hell. He notes that historically across America, there would be big revivals where many, many people come to Christ. Unfortunately, only a few months later, they are nowhere to be found. Ray Comfort attributes this to the fact that the realities of sin and hell are often absent from these events.

He used this analogy to explain this phenomenon well. Pretend you were on a plane and wanted to pass out parachutes to the passengers. To some people, when you give them the parachute, you tell them that it will make their flight so much better. As long as they are holding onto the parachute, they will have so much fun, an absolutely amazing time. These passengers may be excited initially, but what will happen over time? The parachute is big, bulky, and uncomfortable to carry. After a while they will stop holding onto it, letting it go for the sake of comfort. After all, there seems to be no real need for it. What if afterwards, you passed out parachutes to those who did not get one the first time. This time, instead of explaining how amazing their flight will be, you tell them the truth about why they need it. "You will be forced out of this plane at any random moment. If you want to survive, you will need this parachute." How would that person treat the parachute? Would they abandon it once it became uncomfortable? Not at all! They would cling onto that parachute for dear life and never let it go.

Friends, if someone truly understands the wrath of God they face for their sins, as well as the amazing grace shown to them through the cross, it is doubtful they would ever walk away. So many high schoolers and college students walk away from God every year, and I predict that much of it has to do with the fact that they were given a parachute for the sake of a comfortable flight. Do we not want people to cling to Christ? Do we not want people to hold onto the cross like their life depends on it? Do we not want people to have such amazing and eternal hope that no earthly temptation could cause them to walk away? Is that not our goal? Is not our goal to raise up Christians and instill in them a faith that will last? Are we tired of seeing people abandon Christ? I know that I am tired. Yet, when we see people abandon God, we never point to the content of our message. We scramble to make excuses about how the church must not have been modern enough, the worship songs were not trendy enough, or the pastor was not charismatic enough.

Is it so surprising that everyone abandons the parachute, when we never actually communicated why they need to hold onto it? Sure, we may place the doctrines of sin and hell on a corner of our church website. We may say that "I mentioned the word sin once" and conclude that we did our part. Nonetheless, technically believing something is far different from communicating that belief. Believing in the righteous judgment of God on sin is far different than telling others about the righteous judgment of God on sin. We can give people a parachute, telling them that it will feel wonderful to wear, to hold, and to post about in their social media circles, mumbling under our breath that they will have to jump at any moment. "But I technically said it. Therefore, I did our part." And when people walk away from Christ, we wonder why the truth did not sink into their hearts, though we downplayed it and hid it from them the whole time.

Sugarcoated Warnings Are Not Real

One truth that we must come to realize is that sugarcoated warnings are not real warnings. Unless we use honest and straightforward language about sin, we will not be properly warning others about the dangers of sin, or their eternal state without Christ. Imagine you were trying to warn someone about the dangers of driving under the influence. One option would be to tell them that "if this is the path you decide to take, there is a chance that a negative outcome occurs." Or you could be honest and tell them that "this choice may kill you and those around you." The first warning is not a real warning. The second one is. Similarly, imagine if you had a young child who was running into a busy street. What would your reaction be? It would be to shout quickly, "Hey! Get back here!" Only a careless parent would gently say, "hey buddy, I think you should consider coming back to the sidewalk. The street is a bit busy, so you may get a little bit hurt." That would be reckless and criminally negligent. Yet, this is what many preachers do when they sugarcoat hard truths about sin and hell behind light, airy, and inoffensive language.

Tobacco companies as well as e-cigarette companies, have experienced lawsuit upon lawsuit because of their advertisements. They have been accused of giving misleading advertisements that did not truly expose the dangers that come from their products. Tobacco companies have even been found denying the dangers of smoking. These were historic lawsuits that the public rallied behind. After all, these companies did not properly explain the addictiveness and danger of their products, and many were hurt as a result.

The nature of a warning reflects the nature of the danger. When talking about sin, we must convey that danger. Maybe people would heed our warnings if we actually explained what we were warning them about. Maybe we would experience a modern-day revival, with tens of thousands coming to repentance, if we were truthful with people about why they should repent.

When we preach the truth, when we give a proper warning that is not hidden behind pointless euphemisms and obscurations of the truth, it will sting. When coming to Christ, people inevitably must humble themselves to admit that they are sinners in need of a savior. This humbling experience can be quite uncomfortable, yet it results in overflowing and everlasting life. The church today is so scared of humbling others with the truth, even though we know what amazing things await on the other side of that experience. When we preach the truth, though it may sting in the moment, a person brought to Christ is a priceless reward. Why do we fear this sting when we know what it results in? Why do we sugarcoat the warning that could save someone's life?

Sugarcoating the truth about sin and hell may sound nice, but it will also stop people from grasping the truth. If they do not grasp the truth about why they need to repent and trust in Christ, they may die and go to hell thinking they were truly saved. These endless sugar-coatings and nicer retellings of harsh Christian truths are like sweet honey to the ears but poison to the soul. These words may sound nice and gentle and intellectual and modern and whatever other benefit one can come up with, but if they intentionally obscure the truth and hinder others from understanding it, then they are nothing more than deadly poison which does nothing other than deceive and destroy.

Hiding the Gospel Behind Euphemisms

I will admit, it is not technically incorrect to say that we are "broken" or that Christ "restores us" or that His death "gives us new life." These can be helpful words used to further explain the gospel and the work of Christ. The danger appears, though, when one set of words permanently replaces words like sin, repentance, and hell. When an illustration of the truth replaces the truth, the illustration has become a lie. We should strive to avoid all misconceptions that could be made while sharing the gospel. Through overuse of light and flowery language, we risk giving people a misconception about Christ and what the gospel is. What a deadly misconception to have! There was a conversation I had with a spiritual leader placed above me in which I asked for words like sin, repentance, and hell to be used so that the gospel could be presented effectively to those we desired to serve. The response I received was along the lines of: "I believe we do present the gospel, but with different language than you are used to." What was this different language in question? Words like brokenness, restoration, and new life.

Let us compare two different gospel presentations. One will use the words sin, repentance, and forgiveness of sins. The other will use brokenness, restoration, and new life. The latter would go along the lines of "if you turn to Christ, He will restore your brokenness and provide you with new life." The former would be along the lines of "if you turn to Christ and repent, your sins will be wiped away and you will be forgiven." Only one of these messages can convey the gospel without risk of misconception. Only one of these has ever been regarded as too harsh and too blunt. Are we really going to risk someone understanding the gospel over a personal word preference? As we find endless new ways to say things, and excitingly beautiful phrases to use, people are dying in sin while we refuse to say, "your sins will lead you to hell, repent and trust in Christ." I believe that author Barbara Brown Taylor explains this well in her book *Speaking on Sin*, when she writes that "abandoning the language of sin will not make sin go away. Human beings will continue to experience alienation, deformation, damnation and death no matter what we call them. Abandoning the language will simply leave us speechless before them and increase our denial of their presence in our lives. Ironically, it will also weaken the language of grace, since the full impact of forgiveness cannot be felt apart from the full impact of what has been forgiven."

When speaking of things related to sin and repentance, we should use the language that the Bible uses. When Jesus went into Galilee, He said "The time has come … the kingdom of God has come near. Repent and believe the good news!" (Mark 1:15). Jesus also tells a group of people that "unless you repent, you too will all perish" (Luke 13:5). When speaking about fear,

Christ says to "not be afraid of those who kill the body but cannot kill the soul. Rather, be afraid of the One who can destroy both soul and body in hell" (Matthew 10:28). It seemed as though Jesus was straight forward when conveying His message. Many Christians today shy away from phrases and statements like that, even though they were things Christ Himself said.

Euphemisms are often used to obscure the harsh realities of what we are trying to describe. Many times, this is done not only for the sake of the listener but for the sake of the speaker as well. Many are uncomfortable saying that a person died, so they shift the language to "passing away." Expressing dislike may seem rude, so we refer to things as "not being our favorite." Are we striving to deny the realities of sin and hell through our euphemisms? Is our non-abrasive language actually an attempt to obscure something we wish was not real? Do we ourselves struggle to believe these realities, and hide them behind our happy language as a result? As Christians, we believe that if someone dies in sin, they face the eternal judgment of God in a place called hell. No words have ever been able to truly describe what hell will be like, for how can one accurately depict the eternal wrath of almighty God? Knowing this, truly knowing this about hell, how can we stand to obscure this reality from those to whom we speak? How selfish must we be to hide the truth from others because it falls poorly on our own ears?

Now, many may be skeptical of me. They may argue that we do not need to use words such as sin, repentance, and hell, that words such as brokenness, separation, and restoration will do the trick. If that is you, please hear me out. Is it possible that these words are leading to genuine misunderstandings among your listeners? Is it possible for some to take a false gospel away from what you are saying? I do not believe that different language is bad, or that it should be done away with. But could you agree, even for a second, that overuse of non-confrontational language may result in believers who do not repent and are not aware of their sinfulness? Is it impossible to say that Satan rejoices over misunderstandings and misrepresentations of the gospel? Are we to be so naïve as to assume our word choice does not actually matter and that Satan will not use any opportunity he gets to lead others astray? We know that our "enemy the devil prowls around like a roaring lion looking for someone to devour" (1 Peter 5:8). Satan is not opposed to people hearing about "a gospel," only "*the* gospel." Hell rejoices over misrepresentations and misunderstandings of the gospel because it creates a false assurance of heaven supported by a false gospel that cannot save. Satan will let people "have their brokenness made new" or "enter into a grand story of reconciliation," as long as they never repent and trust in Christ.

The false gospel most often conveyed through use of easy-to-hear, non-confrontational language is that of a self-improvement focused Christianity. Think about it. "Jesus came down to restore our brokenness, so that we may be restored and experience a newness of life." This may be an accurate statement to say in light of the true gospel, but the situation looks dire if this is meant to be a gospel presentation on its own. For most people, brokenness and restoration do not equate to sin and forgiveness. Many likely would hear this and think, "yes, I am not a perfect person. I am glad Jesus came to help me overcome my imperfections and cause my life to have more joy. This is the brokenness and restoration the preacher spoke of." You may think this claim is absurd, that no one would interpret it this way. Please, hear my plea. Is it possible that many Christians today are walking around with this gospel, believing that Christ and Christianity are no more than a means of self-improvement, happy lives, and heaven at the end of it all? Is it possible that the language we use leads people to that conclusion? Would our language hinder people from understanding their need to repent? And by hindering people from understanding repentance, have we put their eternity at stake?

A Sacrifice No Longer Remains

If anyone is still skeptical about why we should be blunt about sin, bringing about genuine repentance, look no further than the book of Hebrews. The author tells us that "if we deliberately keep on sinning after we have received the knowledge of the truth, no sacrifice for sins is left, but only a fearful expectation of judgment and of raging fire that will consume the enemies of God" (Hebrews 10:26-27). If we go on sinning deliberately after receiving the truth, that puts into question our salvation. Hebrews is not speaking about the fact that we continue to sin. If so, then none of us would be saved. Rather, it is speaking on those who would know what God requires, then in their heart reject that in order to pursue sin. It is an intentional and internal rejection of God in favor of sin, a choice to live in unrepentant sin.

Shortly after this verse, we are provided with another harsh question, asking "how much more severely do you think someone deserves to be punished who has trampled the Son of God underfoot, who has treated as an unholy thing the blood of the covenant that sanctified them, and who has insulted the Spirit of grace?" (Hebrews 10:29). This condemnation brought about is even harsher, with the charge that these people trample underfoot the Son of God and have insulted the Spirit of grace. This is a grim picture being painted. Those who know about Christ yet reject Him in their lives by ignoring God's call to live for Him not only put into question their salvation, but also are described as those who insult Christ and His sacrifice.

Does this sound anything like the world we live in? Are there those who profess Christ, yet day in and day out intentionally and knowingly live for sin? The Bible gives us horrifically dire warnings about these people, and they are to be found in our personal lives and church congregations. Do we not believe it appropriate to mention these verses? Do we not believe that we should give them this warning? The Bible pulls no punches and does not shy away from harsh realities about these people. How many people would turn back to Christ if given this warning? Our churches, our Christian communities, our Christian universities, are filled with those who reject Christ's rule over their life yet believe that they are still in the right with God. Many are unaware of the reality they face, that they are not right with God. There are many who genuinely believe that their eternity is safe. Will we let them live with this deception? Is that truly the path we want to take?

If we do not preach this reality, if we do not speak on the dangers of pursuing and living in unrepentant sin, we turn Christ into nothing more than a means of fire insurance. You do whatever you want, reject God however you want, then cash out your policy when your life ends. There exist multitudes upon multitudes of self-professing Christians who believe that because they said a specific prayer once when they were seven years old, it does not matter how they spend the rest of their lives. How many churchgoers have lives that utterly mock God and His commandments, yet go to sleep confident that their check-the-box formula means that they can reject God for the rest of their lives? It is verses like Hebrews 10:26 that give us a harsh reminder that faith is not merely intellectual agreement with a list of facts about God. After all, the Bible says that "even the demons believe that [there is one God]" (James 2:19). The devil believes all the right facts about Christ. He believes that Christ is the one true son of God, who lived a sinless life, died to bear the sins of the world, and that all those who repent and trust in Him will be saved. Every demon in existence would agree with that statement. All the while, the demons still reject Christ.

There are a tragically large number of professing Christians today who believe all the correct things about who Jesus is yet reject Him in their hearts. They despise God's teachings and refuse to kneel at the foot of the cross. And in all of this they still think, "I will be alright because I believe this set of facts." Frank Turek, apologist and well-renowned author, put it this way. Intellectual assent is like believing that air travel is safe. True belief and surrender is like flying on the plane. How many lives would change if we preached this truth? If we honestly showed others what the Scripture says about rejecting God with one's life, how many would turn around? How many lives of intellectual agreement would turn to heartfelt surrender if we simply warned people that agreeing with facts is not the same as clinging to the Savior? How many people are we watching speed down the road to hell, believing they are safe, because our fear of offending stops us from telling them otherwise?

Fervor-less Preaching and Poorly Raised Generations

Besides putting the eternity of others at stake, ignoring sin and hell has led to watered down sermons and unconvincing preachers. In general, when we are passionate about a topic, it will come through in our speech. When we give presentations as students, we always do better when the topic is something we are interested in. When a friend asks us about a hobby we love, we excitedly jump on the opportunity to share. This same fervor applies to preaching as well. When a minister is convicted and excited to share the message God has placed on their heart, the excitement comes across, whether that be a message on God's love, or on holy living, or on our assurance in Christ. This enthusiasm especially comes through when the minister believes the topic is important. If the message is important, they will be extra fervent in preaching. After all, there is a strong desire for the congregation to understand what God has to share. Unfortunately, when preaching the gospel, this fervor is not present in many preachers.

It could be that we have lost fervor in preaching because we have lost urgency in message. Almost no one can share the realities about sin and hell without having their heart behind the message. No one can call sinners to repentance without a genuine desire to see people saved. No revivalist ever begged, "I plead with you, be made complete through the renewing restoration of Christ." No open-air preacher pleads with their crowds to "embrace the newness of life Christ has for you." The greatest cries, the most heartfelt sermons, the moments where a preacher's heart is put out for all to see, is when they beg people to see "the Lamb of God who takes away the sin of the world!" (John 1:29). Now, the previously mentioned phrases may very well be good to include in a message. They may very well be important for the congregations to hear. Nonetheless, we cannot expect to bring others to Christ without genuinely understanding their dire need for Christ and conveying that to them. We cannot truly understand one's need for Christ without that coming through in our preaching.

The consequences of euphemized preaching and ignoring hard topics go beyond the four walls of the church building. Throughout life, it is easy to see how many people are the product of their upbringing. Many individuals adopt their beliefs from their parents. Oftentimes one's social skills are a result of how they were raised when they were young. Many people have their worldview impacted by their peers and their education. Similarly, many people's faith is the product of their spiritual upbringing. Because of this, what we teach and speak about now will shape the Christian landscape of the future. The faith we present to others will be the faith that they carry into the world. Because of this, it is important that we do not ignore important doctrines.

If we fail to speak on God's love, we will breed a generation of Christians who do not believe in a loving God. If we fail to give God's heart for the hurting its proper place, we will have a group of believers who fail to live out God's call to help those in need. Similarly, if we slowly erase the doctrines of sin and hell from Christianity, the end result will be Christians who do not believe in hell nor the need for repentance. This becomes ever more dangerous when we think about non-believers coming to the faith. New Christians are sponges when it comes to Christianity. For those who are eager to learn and are excited about Jesus, they will pursue knowledge and consume information at a surprisingly fast rate. As a spiritual resource, the church will help form the foundation of their faith. Even if doctrines like sin and hell are ones we believe, no good is done if we hide these beliefs and forbid them from coming to light.

This is comparable to having a close friend or spouse, and learning something important about them after years of close connection. Imagine learning after ten years of marriage that your spouse has no living family members, yet you spent endless time asking to meet them. Or, what if you took your best friend to a sushi restaurant for their birthday, only to just then learn that they are allergic to fish. The information was always present, but because you did not know it, you did not live by it. Similarly, though we may technically hold the doctrines of sin and hell, unless we make them clear, those we seek to invest in spiritually will not know them. If they do not know them, then they will not live by them. It is a scary thing to imagine professing Christians living as if their own sinfulness and God's punishment on sin are non-existent, all because those truths were never explained.

I can imagine that there is a three-step process by which doctrines disappear from the church. We begin with Christians and ministers who believe in a doctrine, and actively communicate that doctrine. The second generation believes in that doctrine, but refuses to communicate it out of fear or an effort to "draw more people in." The third generation did not hear the doctrine, so they do not believe in those truths or let those truths shape their lives. It does not matter how strongly the second generation believed in those truths if they are destined to remain uncommunicated. There are many up and coming ministers and Christian leaders who fall into the category of the "third generation."

I am terrified of all the new youth pastors, young adult pastors, children's pastors, Christian thinkers and authors, whose ministry is void of any notion of man's sinfulness and God's wrath on sin. These ministers will never call anybody to repent, because they do not believe it to be necessary themselves! Why throw yourself at the foot of the cross and ask Christ for forgiveness if you are not a sinner and forgiveness isn't needed? Why spread the gospel if other people do not face a dreadful eternal fate without Christ? There is a generation of Christian ministers being raised with an absence of belief in hell and man's sinfulness, which will not only destroy any gospel presentation they try to make, but will render their ministry to be nothing more than endless repetitions of "God loves you" and "let's make the world a better place."

Now, there are those who will likely jump on the opportunity to critique me. "Can't people just find these concepts in their Bible? Why is it our job to teach them about these things?" There will be many who argue that in ministry and church contexts, we can focus on the positive, happy, and uplifting ideas, and let the harsher concepts like sin and hell be discovered on one's own time. Mindsets like these severely underestimate the impact that those in spiritual leadership have on others. Yes, people can discover doctrines of sin and hell on their own, but what mindset will they adopt when these ideas are ignored by all of those they look up to? If it appears as if my pastors and spiritual leaders do not believe in hell, why would I believe in it? If it seems like everyone around me does not believe in the sinfulness of man, what is pushing me to do so? Yes, I may discover these themes in the Bible, but what is to stop me from just writing them off as irrelevant or "it doesn't mean what it appears to mean"?

Uncovering these truths in God's Word will bring about cognitive dissonance for people who are surrounded by those who hide or reject these beliefs. To resolve this dissonance, one would either have to reject God's Word or reject the faith community around them, and many people are quick to reject God's Word or "creatively reinterpret" it. If nobody around me believes in hell, when I encounter Scripture that speaks on hell, I will just conclude that it is metaphorical. If nobody around me believes in the sinfulness of man, when the Bible speaks on this very truth, I will tell myself that it is only speaking about our capacity to sin, not an innate tendency or desire.

Furthermore, those who resort to the critique of "people will learn those things on their own" woefully reject their responsibility as ministers, pastors, and ambassadors of Christ. Are we really going to propose that we should wait for our congregation to discover their need to repent? Instead of preaching about the eternal fate of unrepentant sinners, are we really going to ignore it and hope people figure it out on their own? How tragic that there are genuinely people like this in positions of spiritual leadership! Furthermore, what about the unbelievers? What about those who are trying to understand what Christianity is about? Do we not care about presenting non-believers with the truth, or do we expect them to buy a Bible and figure it all out on their own?

Only with a foundation of the gospel, which includes repentance and forgiveness in Christ, can anything else in Christianity truly make sense. The foundation of repentance and forgiveness can only be laid if the realities of sin and hell are understood. Many false gospels and faults of modern Christianity have found their rise due to a shaky foundation in doctrine. Liberation theology flourished when people treated Jesus as a social liberator rather than a savior. Once sin was discarded from our vocabulary, Christ's role as a savior disappeared too, and His role as social justice warrior sped to take its place. Prosperity gospel flourished when God's greatest blessing to us was no longer the cross. The cross was no longer our greatest blessing when we ceased to internalize our deep sinfulness and deep need of a savior.

There are great misunderstandings of faith happening all throughout the west. There are those who believe that good works are a prerequisite for salvation (as opposed to being a fruit of salvation), or that loving others equates to affirming whatever they say and do. Like previously mentioned, there are those who believe that Christ's main goal on Earth was to teach us how to love one another. All of these wrong beliefs, and many more, flourish when the gospel is not at the center of our faith. We believe works are needed to be saved when we forget that we are sinners saved by grace and grace alone. We believe that love equates to affirmation when we forget that because sin is a very real thing we need to be saved from, we should not affirm it. We turn social improvement into Christ's true goal when we abandon the cross and what it actually means. When sin and hell are abandoned as doctrines, the gospel is abandoned as well. Wherever the gospel is abandoned, terrible things inevitably follow. If we abandon the gospel, any resemblance of Christianity that remains is nothing more than deadly poison to the soul.

Conclusion

Ignoring the key doctrines of sin and hell are catastrophic. So is endlessly euphemizing them to the point of unrecognizability. We are all sinners in need of a savior. We must not hide that truth from those we are speaking to. To do that would be to intentionally jeopardize their souls over fear of sounding too harsh. How pitiful we have become, where sounding nice takes precedence over one's eternal fate. To euphemize the gospel would be to destroy it and strip it of its saving power. Not only does this abandonment of sin and hell leave us silent as multitudes march toward hell, but it cripples the church as well. It is quite terrible to hide doctrines of sin and hell, but it is even worse for an entire Christian generation to not hold those beliefs at all! We need to talk about sin and hell honestly for what they are, for both the sake of the church and the sake of the lost.

Chapter 6

Addressing Counter Arguments

At this moment, I would like to address some counter arguments likely to be brought up by some who are reading this book. Some may accuse me of scaring people into repentance, of turning Christianity into nothing more than avoiding hell, of suggesting that every mention of sin should be in a fire and brimstone context, or believing that every sermon should be about sin and repentance. Hopefully these concerns are properly addressed in the following pages.

Scare Tactics

Among those who are opposed to the ideas laid out in this book will be those who accuse me of using scare tactics. They may reason that my desire is to use fear and emotional manipulation in order to bring others to Christ. It seems villainous to scare people into repentance. Unfortunately, this line of thought falls apart in an instant, for the sole reason that the truth is in fact scary. If we share the truth with people, we will invoke fear. That is hardly the same as employing a scare tactic, and to call it such would be intentionally disingenuous. The truth is that those who do not repent will face the eternal judgment and wrath of an all holy and all righteous God. That is an utterly terrifying reality, yet it is the truth. And throughout history, understanding that scary reality has brought many people to Christ.

Imagine that there is a doctor who is trying to administer medication to his patient. Without that medicine, the patient will undergo terrible pain and suffering until the time that he dies. The doctor then relays this information to the patient. "You need to take this medicine. Without it, you will experience misery upon misery for the rest of your life." If any patient heard this, what would they do? Would they accuse the doctor of fear mongering? Would they say that this is a scare tactic to manipulate him into taking the medicine? No! They would take that medicine as fast as they could, because the scary yet honest truth pushed them to the hope found in the solution. The same is true with Christianity.

Now, there are those who do use fear to paint a poor picture of God. This is something unfortunate that has happened throughout church history, in which God is made out to be someone who is heartless, without love, and one who angrily looks down on those pleading for mercy. There are genuine and unfortunate tales of youth groups who would lock up students and yell at them until they all repented. It is quite tragic that there are many who were given the mindset that God does not love them and will strike them down the instant they make a mistake. I grieve for those people. Luckily, that is not the truth about God. As believers who are forgiven, we know that we stand righteous before God and do not need to have this fear. Though lies have been used to spark fear, that does not make the truth any less scary, and that does not make speaking the truth a scare tactic. If speaking about eternal damnation is a scare tactic, if mentioning the wrath of God is a scare tactic, if warning about the consequences of sin is a scare tactic, then the Bible is full of God using scare tactics. The prophets time and time again spoke of God's wrath that would be poured out on sinful nations. Are we going to say that the prophets unfairly used fear? No! They spoke the truth about what was going to happen, and the truth was scary. Their primary goal was not to incite fear, but to speak the truth, which in turn brought about fear in those who heard. The truth is scary, and that is something modern Christians need to accept. Hell is scary. God's wrath is scary. The Bible says that "anyone whose name was not found written in the book of life was thrown into the lake of fire" (Revelation 20:15). The Lake of Fire sounds quite terrifying. If you do not want to risk sparking fear in others, then you cannot speak the truth. The truth about what happens to unrepentant sinners is utterly terrifying. Accept that fact. And as a Christian, if the concept of your unsaved friends and family spending eternity in eternal darkness and punishment does not invoke at least a little bit of fear in you, you need to seriously reexamine your heart.

Throughout all of Scripture, knowledge of God's righteous judgment on sin, and fear of experiencing that judgment, has brought people into repentance. When Jonah preached to Nineveh what they would face for their sins, what happened? The king made a decree for everyone to "call urgently on God. Let them give up their evil ways and their violence. Who knows? God may yet relent and with compassion turn from his fierce anger so that we will not perish" (Jonah 3:8-9). In the parable of the tax collector and the pharisee, the tax collector knowing his sinful status cries out "God, have mercy on me, a sinner!" (Luke 18:13), and Jesus called this man justified in God's eyes. While Israel was in the wilderness, "they spoke against God and against Moses, and said, 'Why have you brought us up out of Egypt to die in the wilderness? There is no bread! There is no water! And we detest this miserable food!'" (Numbers 21:5). God judged them that moment, and "sent venomous snakes among them; they bit the people and many Israelites died" (Numbers 21:6). The Israelites experienced in real time the judgment of God for their sin, and what happened? They repented, came to Moses and said that "we sinned when we spoke against the Lord and against you. Pray that the Lord will take the snakes away from us" (Numbers 21:7). Time and time again, the Bible shows us that understanding man's sinfulness and God's punishment of sin leads people to repentance. We do not have examples that show us otherwise.

When we convey the truth about God's judgment, we are not artificially trying to invoke fear. We are not exaggerating in order to get a response. Parents oftentimes try to scare their kids into avoiding certain actions or behaviors. Even if there are valid reasons to avoid that behavior, parents easily exaggerate in order to get their desired result. Many parents will tell their kids that holding hands will lead to pregnancy, that turning the light on in the car will cause the cops to arrest them, or that forgetting to brush your teeth once means that they will all fall out. In all these instances, the consequences are magnified and blown out of proportion to result in the desired behavior. That is not what we are doing when we speak of God's judgment on sin in order to bring people into repentance. We are not exaggerating in order to bring people to Christ. We are not lying in order to scare them. We are simply telling them the truth, and the truth is scary.

The hope that is found in the gospel will always outweigh the fear of eternal punishment. Those who claim that speaking on hell is a scare tactic conveniently seem to forget how joyous and wonderful salvation is. Any fear brought about through speaking the truth can also be replaced with hope by speaking the truth that Christ suffered the punishment we deserved, so that all who repent and trust in Him will be saved. This begs the question over whether these "anti-fear" people even know the gospel for themselves. If they truly knew and understood the gospel, they would not be afraid of invoking fear, because they would know that this fear would be replaced in an instant through the good news of Jesus Christ.

Is the Only Point of Christianity to Avoid Hell?

Another accusation I am likely to get is that I am minimizing other aspects of the faith by magnifying the issues of sin and God's punishment of sin. "God cares about so much more than just getting us to heaven. He cares about justice, loving our neighbor, and transforming our lives through joy and peace. Are you just going to forget about those and endlessly speak about what terrible sinners we are?" Some may accuse me of turning Christianity into simply a means of avoiding hell, and minimizing everything else that Christ has to offer for our lives. If this is a belief you hold about me, I would like to address it now.

One, I do not deny how Christianity extends far past the forgiveness of sins. The Bible speaks extensively of the inner transformation God does in our lives. We know that God desires justice in the world, that He has a powerful love for us, and that He desires unity among His people. To deny the existence of these things would be improper for a Christian. Yet, these things can only be properly understood in the light of the gospel. The gospel forms the foundation and the center of our faith, and as we have seen, one cannot have the proclamation of the gospel without acknowledging the sinful state of man and God's wrath on sin. Our theology and faith cannot be properly understood or lived out without a proper understanding of the gospel. Without the gospel, we cannot properly understand Christ. We cannot properly follow Jesus and cannot properly experience the life He has for us without a foundation that includes His love for us, and His death and resurrection to save us from the consequences of our sin. Christianity is infinitely more than just sin and hell, but it is not less than that.

Furthermore, this book specifically centers around sin and hell because those are topics surprisingly absent from contemporary Christian culture. If the church abandoned speaking on God's love, one would write a book on that. If the church forgot about caring for others, that would be something to sound the alarm over. It is not that Christians should only care about sin and repentance, yet a renewed emphasis needs to be made about a doctrine that is slowly being forgotten and minimized. As we have seen previously, the gospel is the center of the Christian faith. Without a healthy understanding of sin, we cannot have a healthy understanding of the gospel. If we remove the gospel from Christianity, we cannot have the Jesus of the Bible. If we do not have the Jesus of the Bible, we do not have Jesus.

In line with the previous critique, some may also believe that by an entire book dedicated to talking about sin, I may believe all sermons should be about sin. Some may falsely believe that I am against any sermon that is not about the sinfulness in our lives or how wretched we are or how we need to repent. This is not the case. I do not wish to overcorrect and make every sermon a fire and brimstone message about sin. That would be equally as bad. Nonetheless, I believe that the modern church has gone too far in one direction and abandoned most talk and language surrounding sin, our sinfulness, and hell. The church is full of love but no justice, grace but no wrath, being saved but ignoring what we are saved from.

The Bible is full of things to preach about. After all, the Bible covers a multitude of topics and is relevant as well as authoritative in all areas of our lives that it addresses. It teaches us about how God is the creator of the world. It teaches us practical wisdom for life. It gives us a model for marriage and sexuality. These are all things that should be covered in church. It would be almost comical to ignore all these things to solely talk about sin. Rather, the danger that I want to highlight is the intentional exclusion of certain truths in order to artificially present a contrived image of the faith. Not every message has to be about sin, but if no message includes talk about sin, it would be because we are intentionally and systematically avoiding it.

Does Every Message Have to be Fire and Brimstone?

A common misconception that many people believe is that speaking about concepts like sin and hell would make every message a "fire and brimstone" sermon. We may think of the stereotypical preacher who spends their time yelling at the congregation and creating a sense of hopelessness in the listeners. This is an unfortunate stereotype, but in order to avoid it many have overcorrected and avoided mentioning sin and hell altogether. Mentioning sin and hell in a sermon does not always have to be bleak and harsh. After all, mentioning the sinful things of the world provides a great opportunity to highlight the blessings of doing things God's way. Speaking on the gift of married sexuality provides an opportunity to mention the destructiveness that comes from twisting God's design. Speaking about the evils of abortion can show the congregation how the image of God is present in all people. Mentioning our terrible fate without Christ is an opportunity to emphasize the amazing grace God gives us through the cross.

Truthfully, we cannot speak about living for God unless we speak about how *not* to live for God. We cannot speak about God's holiness unless we also speak about what that holiness excludes. Calls to avoid sin and live more faithfully for Christ do not always have to be the 1800's fire and brimstone stereotype that we imagine. Admittedly, pastors like that do exist. There are pastors who will preach no love and grace, only the wrath of God. This is extremely harmful and maligns the character of God greatly. Though it is disappointing that many churches preach love without truth, it is equally disappointing that many churches preach truth without love. History could point to many examples, both modern and historic, where pastors would spend a sermon breaking down the hearts of their listeners, and then end the message. The congregants would leave feeling ashamed, heartbroken, utterly contemptible, and without any hope. Leaving people like this is a great disservice, and many of those who listened to this type of preaching have become disillusioned and abandoned the faith altogether. What good preachers do, contrarily, is speak the harsh and honest truth about sin while also providing hope through the proclamation of grace. When speaking on sin and the need to repent, there is a certain amount of sting that is unavoidable. After all, those who listen will be confronted with their own imperfections and how they fall short before an all-mighty and all-holy God. This sting is unavoidable, yet it is soothed by grace. As the sinner is broken down over their sense of sinfulness, they are uplifted through the good news that there is a loving God who died to pay the price for their sins and bring them into right relationship with Him.

Johnathan Edwards is a notable preacher and author, and one involved in the "Great Awakening" of America in the 1700s. One of Jonathan Edwards most notable recorded sermons is entitled *Sinners in the Hand of an Angry God*. The sermon is available to read online, and when reading it one can see how bluntly yet truthfully Edwards explains the condition of sinners, God's wrath to be poured out on sin, and the eternal state of the sinner who does not trust in Christ. Though the message is disliked by some and found to portray God in too angry of a light, none can deny the influence it had during the Great Awakening. For all the language of fire and brimstone

Edwards used, he did not leave listeners in despair. At the end of his message, he calls his listeners to come to Christ, saying that:

> "now you have an extraordinary opportunity, a day wherein Christ has thrown the door of mercy wide open, and stands in calling and crying with a loud voice to poor sinners; a day wherein many are flocking to him, and pressing into the kingdom of God. Many are daily coming from the east, west, north and south; many that were very lately in the same miserable condition that you are in, are now in a happy state, with their hearts filled with love to him who has loved them, and washed them from their sins in his own blood, and rejoicing in hope of the glory of God."

Edwards tactics and speaking style might not be the proper choice in all instances, yet I believe his famous sermon still serves as an important example for Christians today. We might not need to spend one hour detailing the horrors of hell and God's wrath, but we should also not ignore that truth. Any despair, guilt, or sense of insufficiency stirred up in the listener can always be soothed by the good news of the gospel. Friends, I love talking about the grace of God. It is the most powerful thing in the world. The gospel is the greatest news of all time and forms the core of our faith. Nonetheless, we cannot properly talk about the grace of God until we lay the foundation of why we need that grace. We cannot speak about the joys of salvation until we explain what we are saved from. Christ's forgiveness cannot be properly expounded upon until we establish what we are forgiven from. While the gospel is not about fire and brimstone, the reality of hell lays the foundation for the extraordinary life-changing grace that is found in the gospel.

Conclusion

As shown, many of the counter arguments to speaking about sin and hell fall utterly short. While genuine fear has been used as a weapon in the past, truthfully speaking on the fearful reality of hell is no more a scare tactic than a doctor truthfully speaking on the fearful reality of a disease. Furthermore, Christianity is much, much more than a means of avoiding hell, yet sin and hell are specifically emphasized in this book due to their unfortunate absence in much of contemporary Christianity. When speaking on sin and hell, it does not have to be done in a fire and brimstone manner. Nonetheless, even with the kindest and gentlest pastor, the realities of sin and hell cannot be denied. Finally, though Christianity is a deep, expansive, and rich faith, we cannot elevate certain truths to the exclusion of others.

Conclusion

It Does Matter

As we have seen, we need to talk about sin. Sin and its punishment are key doctrines of the Christian faith, and one that Christians have become numb too. We live in a sinfully saturated society, so much so that we fail to view sin the way that God sees sin. As sin becomes normalized and vices are turned into virtues, it is important that Christians speak out against sin and take a stand. Furthermore, the doctrines of sin and God's punishment of sin are core to the Christian faith. Themes of sin and our sinfulness are woven everywhere throughout the Bible. Without sin, Christ and the cross become pointless, and the gospel is nothing more than an idle tale. We cannot even begin to properly understand God's great love for us without first understanding our own sinfulness.

We also have a responsibility to convey the whole counsel of God, which includes ideas of sin and hell. We are called to be watchmen for those around us, to convey the Word of God, and to not omit a word. We even get a dire warning from Christ Himself about those who would deny or be ashamed of His words. When we speak of sin and hell, people are convicted. It is this very conviction that causes people to repent and trust in Christ as their Lord and Savior. Because of that, how we speak has real consequences. How we handle (or not handle for that matter) doctrines of sin and hell can very well warp one's understanding of Christianity and affect their eternity.

It may not be popular, and it may not be appealing, but when has following God been either of those things? This is my plea to Christians everywhere. My plea to pastors, to ministers, to those who work in Christian higher education. My plea to the everyday Christian as well. We need to talk about sin. As the world is filled with sin and immorality, and as Christians themselves shy away from hard topics in order to appeal to the masses, let us not follow their example. Let us stand on truth, answer the call of God, and speak honestly about sin and its consequences. Would God help us all.

Acknowledgements

There are many people that I would like to thank in relation to this book. First, I would like to thank the very talented Jenna Bernath for her help in editing this book as well as her willingness to do it on short notice. I would also like to thank Annika Carlander for the helpful feedback she provided as well. I would like to thank my wonderful fiancée Ashley for her overwhelming support and encouragement throughout this entire process, as well as my parents and sister for their encouragement as well. I would also like to express my gratitude to you: the reader. Thank you for purchasing a copy of this book and taking the time to read it. I hope and pray that it was beneficial to you in some way.

Finally, I would like to thank those who have stood by me and supported me during my last two years at Point Loma Nazarene University. In many ways, the heart behind this book started in fall of 2022. The creation of this book has been a product of many battles and personal trials in defense of the biblical truth behind sin, God's punishment of sin, and the life changing grace and forgiveness that is found in the gospel. To those who stood by me and uplifted me in all of that, you have my undying gratitude.

www.ingramcontent.com/pod-product-compliance
Lightning Source LLC
Chambersburg PA
CBHW071331140726
47996CB00005B/1929